BOUNCERS
and
SHAKERS

BOUNCERS

by John Godber

SHAKERS

by John Godber and Jane Thornton

WARNER CHAPPELL PLAYS

LONDON

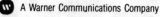 A Warner Communications Company

Bouncers first published 1987 by
Warner Chappell Plays Ltd,
129 Park Street, London W1Y 3FA
Copyright © John Godber, 1987
Shakers first published 1987 by
Warner Chappell Plays Ltd,
129 Park Street, London W1Y 3FA
Copyright © John Godber and Jane Thornton, 1987
ISBN 0 85676 132 X
Second edition 1989

Typeset and printed by Commercial Colour Press, London E7.
Cover design by Robin Lowry.

BOUNCERS

by John Godber

BOUNCERS was originally commissioned and performed by the Yorkshire Actors Company and first performed at the Rotherham Arts Centre on 25 March 1983, with the following cast:

LUCKY ERIC	Peter Geeves
JUDD	John Graham Davies
RALPH	Paul Rhys
LES	Andrew Dunn
MARCIA	Amanda Metro

Direction and production by Andrew Winters

AUTHOR'S NOTE

Bouncers is about working-class Britons at play. It is both a
warning and a celebration. The style is deliberately elliptical
and sharp, necessitating a performance style that depends as
much on energy as it does technique. Fast, clean and rhythmic
movements are married with acute and natural social
observations in order to create a nightmarish vision of the disco
world. *Bouncers* occupies the night-time, and the darker elements
of the play should act as a constant undercurrent.

The play requires strong, physically versatile and above all
flexible actors. This flexibility can be applied to the script. Any
document about recent affairs is clearly in danger of becoming a
museum piece. As a consequence, my own productions of
Bouncers often change in reference, in length and in
temperament. In short, *Bouncers* contains many truths about the
nature of night-life, but one need not necessarily show them all.
The play can run from forty minutes to an hour and a half.
Keep it alive for today. Make it work for your particular actors,
in your particular space, and you will have a first-class
production of *Bouncers*. Directors of the play should never think
of Chekhov; rather, they should think of cartoons and cinematic
techniques. The play was conceived for an audience that
regards the theatre as box sets, big red curtains and tedious
actors. The theatre can certainly be all that — but it can also be
Bouncers.

John Godber
January 1987

photograph by Steve Morgan from the Hull Truck Theatre Company production of Bouncers *at the Donmar Warehouse, 1986.*

Setting: a provincial discotheque. The stage is bare and no props are used apart from a couple of beer kegs and four handbags. During the course of the action, the four bouncers, RALPH, JUDD, LES *and* LUCKY ERIC *portray over thirty different characters. The switches of roles should be fast and sharp, emphasised by music and lighting. Disco music and lighting should be used to full effect to create the atmosphere of the place.*

As the audience enters, the music plays, the lights flash and the bouncers establish the mood of the evening; walking up and down the aisles, generally surveying people, ushering them to their seats, passing the occasional threatening comment, etc. Gradually, they make their way to the stage. We focus in on LUCKY ERIC, *the wise old owl of the bouncers, who addresses the audience in time to the rap which plays in the background.*

ERIC   Ladies and Gentleman...we present *Bouncers.*
        We welcome you to a vision
        Of the eighties urban night life
        To stag nights and hen dos
        To drunken crying girls and gallons of booze
        It's celebration time—come on
        It's always frustrating
        For the oldest swingers in town
        Yes, all human life is inevitably here
        In a midnight circus
        And I must make it clear
        That the beer is pricy, the music pulsating
        The atmosphere is intoxicating
        We four will try and illustrate
        The sort of thing that happens late
        At night in every town
        When the pubs are shut
        And the beer's been downed...

        (LUCKY ERIC *joins the other bouncers in a line across the stage and they begin the rap. They carry out a complicated dance routine as they sing.*)

ERIC   I said a hip hop
        a hippy a hippy
        a hip hip hop and don't you stop

ALL   I said a hip hop
        a hippy a hippy
        a hip hip hop and don't you stop

(They then move straight into the lyrics of the 'Bouncers Rap'. *)

Eric DOWN AT THE DISCO IS THE PLACE TO BE
THE LIGHTS ARE SO BRIGHT
LIKE A COLOURED TV
THE MUSIC IS LOUD
AND THE BEER FLOWS FREE
IT'S A DISCO PLACE FOR YOU AND ME

NOW ON THE DOOR YOU PAY YOUR MONEY
THE PLACE IS PACKED
THE PLACE IS FUNNY
LOOK AT THE GIRLS

All MMMM...

Eric SMELL THEIR HONEY
THEIR HEADS ARE HAZY
LIMBS ARE LAZY
AND ALL THE YOUNG GIRLS DANCE LIKE CRAZY
COME ON
PUT ON YOUR CLOTHES

Judd FROM THE C & A

Eric DO UP YOUR HAIR

Les DOES IT FEEL OK?

Eric I SAID GO

All YES

Eric I SAID GO

All YES

Eric I SAID GO TO THE PLACE THAT IS THE BEST
NOW THE DISCO PLACE
THE DISCO BEAT
IT'S THE KIND OF BEAT
THAT MOVES YOUR FEET
IN THE HEAT

*the 'Bouncers Rap' single is available from Hull Truck Theatre, Spring Street, Hull HU2 8RW. Alternatively, the Sugarhill Gang's 'Rappers Delight' would provide the right rhythm needed.

THE BEAT
YOU CAN'T DEFEAT
IN THE HEAT
THE BEAT
YOU WATCH THE MEAT
YOU WANNA STAY COOL
YOU WANNA STAY NEAT
THE DISCO STREET
THE DISCO BEAT
COME ON
WELL YOU FINISH WORK

ALL   WELL IT'S FRIDAY NIGHT

ERIC   AND YOU'VE GOT YOUR PAY

ALL   SO YOU FEEL ALRIGHT

JUDD   INTO THE PUB

ERIC   WHAT DO YOU DO?

ALL   DOWN EIGHT PINTS

ERIC   YOU DON'T CARE

ALL   COS IT'S FRIDAY NIGHT

ERIC   I SAID HIP HIPPY
         GIP GIPPY
         HIP GIP HOP BOP
         DRINK THAT SLOP

ALL   AND DON'T YOU STOP
         GET DOWN GET UP
         GET IN GET OUT
         GET DOWN GET UP
         GET IN GET OUT
         GET DOWN GET UP
         GET IN GET OUT

JUDD   THE BOUNCERS ARE MEAN IN THEIR
         BLACK AND WHITE

RALPH   THE FELLAS ARE PISSED AND THEIR FISTS
         ARE TIGHT

LES   BUT THE CHICKS ARE LOOSE

ALL   COS IT'S FRIDAY NIGHT

ERIC	WE GOT SOUL
ALL	RAPY
ERIC	WE GOT SOUL
ALL	RAP RAP
ERIC	WE PLAY LOTS OF OTHER STUFF
JUDD	THAT SOUNDS LIKE...(CRAP)
ALL	SHUDDUP GET DOWN GET UP GET IN GET OUT GET DOWN GET UP GET IN GET OUT GET DOWN GET UP GET IN GET OUT
LES	IF YOU COME DOWN HERE WEARING JEANS
JUDD	YOU CAN'T GET IN
ALL	KNOW WHAT HE MEANS GOT TO HAVE A TIE YOU GOTTA HAVE A SUIT YOU GOTTA LOOK CUTE OR YOU'LL GET THE BOOT YOU GOTTA HAVE A TIE YOU GOTTA HAVE A SUIT (*Repeat to fade until only* RALPH *is still singing loudly by himself and looking like a real idiot. Sudden switch to the sound of a telephone ringing.* LES *becomes a smooth-talking radio DJ.*)
LES	You're listening to Radio One with Steve Wright... Hello Steve. It's Gervaise here. Keep your tongue out and I'll call you back. Alright?
ALL	1059. 1083.
LES	Yes. That was *The Bouncers*. Strange name for a group, that one. What do you think, Mr Sinden?
JUDD	(*as if Donald Sinden*) I need alcohol. I need cigarettes, satin knickers and a knighthood. Nobody speaks when I am on stage.

LES	Yes. That record is going down very well in the discos so I shall certainly be playing it tonight at my gig in Littlehampton.
RALPH	Yes indeedy. Dave Doubledex here.
ALL	Get the picture.
JUDD	Let's have that off.

(Suddenly the scene changes and the bouncers become female customers in a ladies hairdresser. RALPH sits under a hair dryer, reading a magazine. ERIC [MAUREEN] is having his hair washed by JUDD [CHERYL]. LES is offstage.)

JUDD	That Steve Wright gets up my ring...and he's so popular because people keep ringing him up. Do you listen to it, Maureen?
ERIC	No, Cheryl love. It gets on my bloody nerves. I like that Bruno Brooks and Gaz za za Davies.
JUDD	This new *Alberto Balsam* should do wonders for your hair, Maureen.
ERIC	Do you think so?
JUDD	Oh yeah.
ERIC	I want to look nice for tonight.
JUDD	Going anywhere special?
ERIC	It's Rosie's twenty-first. It should be a good do.
JUDD	I hope it is, love.
ERIC	You know her. She comes in here. She works at our place. Four of us are going down to *Mr Cinders*.
JUDD	Oh, I've heard some good reports about that place.
ERIC	Yes. It's alright.
ALL	Yes. It's alright.
ERIC	It's the best place round here.
JUDD	It's all plush, isn't it?
ERIC	Yeah. You've got to get there early to get in. It gets packed out. Like the black hole of bloody Calcutta.

(LES *enters the hairdresser out of breath. He has become* ROSIE.)

LES   Chuffin' hell. Talk about being rushed off your feet. Look at the time and I've only just finished.

ERIC   What've you been up to, Rosie?

LES   An order came in at ten to four...

ERIC   Chuffin' cheek.

LES   Friday and all. And my bleeding birthday.

ERIC   Cheeky getts.

LES   Can you fit me in, Cheryl?

JUDD   I can't, I'm afraid, love. I'm chock-a-block till seven.

RALPH   I told her to book.

JUDD   I'm going out myself...*Dragonara Casino.*

ERIC   Gambling?

JUDD   Well...

ERIC   Bloody 'ell.

LES   I'll just have to be late, that's all. I'll nip over to Barbara's. She might be able to fit me in. I'll see you down here later, Maureen.

ERIC   Alright, luv.

LES   Tara, luvs.

ALL   Tara.

LES   Tara everyone.

ERIC   She's a dizzy sod, that Rosie.

RALPH   (*getting uncomfortable under the hairdryer*) How much longer, Cheryl?

JUDD   Bloody hell. She's on fire!!

ERIC   Cheryl.

JUDD   Bloody hell. I wish you'd get your hair cut.

ERIC   I've got a new sort of skirt thing. It's nice, a bit tight, but so what? Ski pants as well.

JUDD	*C & A?*
ERIC	No.
JUDD	*Top Shop?*
ERIC	No chance. Got it from *Chelsea Girl*.
JUDD RALPH }	*Chelsea Girl.*
JUDD	Oh yeah. They're lovely. I've got one in a sort of maroon.
ERIC RALPH }	Maroon.
JUDD	I got them in the sale.
ERIC	How much were they?
ALL	Barbers—

(*Although the scene remains exactly the same we are now in a barbers.* JUDD *is a brusque barber.* ERIC *is in the chair.* RALPH *reads a dirty magazine.*)

JUDD	Come and get your hair cut if you dare.
RALPH	Jesus Christ! Where is he?
ERIC	I can't see him.
JUDD	I'm over here, lads. Right. Who wants what? You young lads want a proper haircut. Well, for a quid you can have the Norman Invader look. Very popular with the thugs. Or for three fifty you can have the Elephant Man cut.
ERIC	What's the Elephant Man cut?
JUDD	It makes one side of your head look bigger than the other.
RALPH	Funny barber.
JUDD	You said it.
RALPH	I wouldn't let him near me.
ERIC	Why?
RALPH	Look at his own hair.

JUDD   (*ignoring them*) Or you can have the Tony Curtis
          haircut look.

ERIC   Hey, what's the Tony Curtis haircut look?

JUDD   All off. Totally bald. Egghead cut.

ERIC   Tony Curtis doesn't have his hair cut like that...

JUDD   He does if he comes in here. Funny, eh? Funny, lads,
          eh?

ERIC   Just cut it, will yer and cut the gags.

          (Eric *gets in the chair and* JUDD *begins to cut his hair.*)

JUDD   Going somewhere, are we?

ERIC   Disco.

JUDD   How old are you?

RALPH   (*looking at a magazine*) Juddy hell! Look at the body on
          that.

ERIC   I'm nineteen.

JUDD   Got a woman?

RALPH   I hope that she's down there tonight.

ERIC   I might have at two o'clock.

JUDD   Make sure that you don't get an ugly one.

RALPH   There's only ugly ones left at two o'clock.

ERIC   Bollocks, Jerry.

JUDD   Watch the language, you.

RALPH   What are you doing to his hair? He can't go out like
          that...hey you can keep away from me, you bleeding
          maniac.

JUDD   Anything on?

ERIC   No thanks. What time are we starting?

RALPH   Time they do open.

          (LES *enters.*)

LES   I'm here, you dreamers.

ERIC   Kev ready for the big night.

LES   Ready as I'll ever be.

RALPH   Hey. I am dying for it. I've starved myself all week.

ERIC   He's a dirty sod.

LES   Seven o'clock in the Taverners, right?

ERIC
RALPH   } Right.

LES   Alright.

ERIC
RALPH   } Alright.

LES   Where's Terry?

JUDD   I'm here.

(JUDD *switches from playing the barber to playing* TERRY. *The scene changes to a street corner where they all wait for* TERRY.)

ALL   I thought he was the barber.

JUDD   Just finished a mindless day of wood stackin', talking about the races at Chepstow, the dogs at White City and the problems of getting Leeds back into Europe...

ALL   (*chant*) United!

JUDD   ...ready for the night-time. Mindless girl watching and a chance perhaps of the old sniff of perfume and feel of inside thigh; milky-white thighs and bloodshot eyes. It's no surprise that I'm dying for it.

ALL   See you down there at seven.

ALL   Terry—Jerry—Kev—Baz—

JUDD   Be young—

ERIC   Be foolish—

LES   But be happy—

ALL   Be da da da da da da da da...

RALPH   And be careful not to catch it!

ALL   Bollocks!

           (*The actors now become the lads getting ready for the big night out.*)

ERIC   Baz, that is it. Friday night, fit for a fight. Get down there. Have a skinful. Might have a Chinese, or a chicken-in-the-basket. Maybe a hot-dog. Might risk it. Got my dole money saved up. Try and pull some skirt. Give her a pup.

RALPH   I'm looking cool. I'm looking great. Wish I didn't have that spot. (*He squeezes an imaginary spot.*) Gotcha!! Blackheads. Slap some *Clearasil* on my face. Not bad, Jerry. Not bad at all, mate.

ERIC   Hope I don't get stabbed again.

JUDD   Time, is it?

LES   Jesus Christ...

RALPH   Ten to seven.

LES   Gonna be late.

RALPH   Time for another quick check.

           (*They all stand in a row and check the various parts of their bodies.*)

ERIC   Hair?

LES   Check.

JUDD   Tie?

LES   Check.

ERIC   Aftershave? Cliff Richard uses this.

ALL   (*sing*) Got myself a sleeping walking...

RALPH   Check.

ERIC   Talc on genitals?

LES   Check.

ERIC   Clean underpants?

RALPH   Well...

LES   They'll do.

Eric	Money?
Judd	Double check.
Les	Condoms?
Eric	Checkaroonie.
Judd	Breath?

(*They all breathe out and try and smell their own breath.*)

All	Ugh! Beer should drown that.
Judd	Right. That's it then. We're ready. Catch the bus at the end of our street.
Ralph	Ding ding.
Les	Fares please.
Eric	Bollocks.
Judd	Get down town to start the pub crawl. When we get there it's packed already. I see me mates. Baz, Jerry an' Kev an' me into the Taverners.

(*During the following sequence the lads attempt to get served. Their actions should convey the bustling, pushy atmosphere of a pub.*)

Judd	Four pints, please!
All	(*as they down the first pint of the evening*) ONE!!
Les	Course I'm eighteen.
Eric	Get some crisps.
Judd	Four bags of beef.
Ralph	Look at tits on that.
All	(*to audience*) Social comment.
Judd	Four pints, pal.
All	TWO!!
Ralph	Hey, who's pushing?
Eric	Are you being served?
Les	Hey up, bastard.
Ralph	Four more pints, pal.

ALL	THREE!!
JUDD	Got any pork scratchings?
ERIC	Hey, watch me shirt.
RALPH	Look who's pushing?
LES	Packed in't it?
JUDD	Let me get to them bogs.
ERIC	Excuse me.
RALPH	Four pints.
ALL	FOUR!!
JUDD	And a whisky, love, please.
ALL	FIVE!!
ERIC	Excuse me, love.
LES	I gave you a fiver.
JUDD	Fat gett.
RALPH	Four pints, four bags of beef, four bags of salted peanuts and four whisky chasers.
ALL	SIX!! SEVEN!!
JUDD	Have you got any cashews?
ERIC	Hey twat, I've been stood here a month.
LES	Can we have some service down here?
RALPH	I'm next, love.
ERIC	Shut your mouth, skullhead.
JUDD	I'm being served, love, thanks.
	(*The four lads recoil as they see beer spill all over* ERIC [BAZ]*'s trousers.*)
ERIC	Oooooh! Look at that. Somebody's spilt beer all over my suit.
JUDD	Daft gett.
ERIC	It's brand new.
LES	It'll dry.

JUDD   How many have we had?

RALPH   Ten.

JUDD   Time for another.

ERIC   I've only had nine.

RALPH   Are we off?

ERIC   D'you think we'll get in?

JUDD   Should do.

LES   Hope there's no trouble.

ERIC   There's four of us.

ALL   Yeah.

RALPH   Come on. Let's get down there, pick something up.
        Right.

ALL   Right.

ERIC   Hang on.

LES   What?

ERIC   Piss call.

ALL   Oh yeah.

        (*They all turn their backs as if peeing and then turn back to
        face the audience.*)

JUDD   We'd better split up.

LES   Why?

JUDD   The Bouncers.

ERIC   Don't let you in. In groups.

RALPH   OK. Me and Kev. Right.

JUDD   Yeah. And me and...(*realising who he's paired off with.*)
        Oh shit!

        (*Just as they are about to move away they all freeze. Pause.
        They once more become the girls we saw earlier in the
        hairdresser sequence.* ERIC [MAUREEN], LES [ROSIE],
        JUDD [ELAINE], *and* RALPH [SUZY] *all stand together in a
        circle having a laugh and a drink in a pub. They are all
        dressed up in their brand new clothes ready for the night out.
        This should be communicated to the audience through their
        actions. They introduce themselves one by one.*)

ERIC	Maureen. Massive but nice. Fat but cuddly. Not a bag, but likes a drink and a laugh. A bit busty.
LES	Rosie. Birthday today. Tall and slim, hair all permed. I had it done at Barbara's.
ERIC	It's nice. It really suits you.
LES	Thank you.
ERIC	Cow.
LES	I've had a drink. I feel a bit tiddly. Hey, it will end in tears. Hello luv.
ERIC	Hello.
LES	Have you lost a bit of weight?
JUDD	Plain Elaine.
ERIC LES	} It's a shame.
JUDD	Left school at sixteen with one CSE in metalwork. I'm on the dole.
ERIC LES	} It's such a shame.
JUDD	Enjoys a good night out but doesn't expect to get picked up though. Handy in a fight...come here ya bastard.
RALPH	Rosie, Maureen, Elaine...
ALL	Suzy...
RALPH	...sexy...I've got stockings on under my dress. Do you wanna look? You cheeky getts! Go on then. Anybody's for half a lager. Goes under the sunbed...brown all over. I bet you would fancy it, big boy. Ooh, he's nice that one.
LES	I'll say he is. Yeah. Right. Who wants what?
JUDD	I'll have a pint of Guinness...no, only a joke. I'll have a brandy and lime.
ERIC	Well. I'll have a lager and black because if I have any more I'll be on my back.
LES	As usual.

ERIC	You cheeky sod.
LES	Sorry.
RALPH	I'll have a *Pina Colada*.
ERIC	Christ. Listen to her.
RALPH	Well I'm eighteen.
LES	She doesn't bloody care. I feel a bit sick.
ERIC	You'll be alright when we get down there.
LES	Are we getting the bus?
RALPH	Well, I'm not walking it in these shoes.
ALL	They're lovely.
RALPH	I know.
JUDD	I'm gonna put a record on.
ALL	Ya da da da da da da ya da da da da.

(JUDD *walks up to an imaginary jukebox, represented by* ERIC. LES *and* RALPH *join* JUDD *around the jukebox.*)

RALPH	Put that on 3A. I like that.
JUDD	No. It's crap.
LES	I think you should put Wham on.
JUDD	I'm putting on a funky disco record.
RALPH	I'm afraid you are not, because I like this one here by Sister Sledge. (*Singing, as if the record*) I was walking down the street one day, I heard a voice, I heard a voice... (*repeats as if the record is sticking.*)

(*Sudden blackout and freeze. The actors walk to the side of the stage. A dark and foreboding sound filters out from the speakers. The pace has been fast and hectic up until this point, but now the stage is quite still. We are outside the club. Eerie, disturbing music plays as we move into a mime sequence during which the bouncers come to life. During this sequence each actor should create and display a kind of larger-than-life character for each bouncer. It is at this point that the individual characteristics of each bouncer are established. Ordinary mannerisms and gestures are grotesquely exaggerated as one by one, the bouncers step forward to introduce themselves through mime.* JUDD, *for example, walks slowly and cautiously to the centre of the stage, looks around, takes a hand exerciser out of his pocket and begins to do a series of exercises. He does so to the point of exhaustion, his face grimacing as the seeping pain of lactic acid invades his forearm muscles. He puts away the exerciser and has a moment's silence to himself. He takes a comb out of his pocket and begins to carefully comb his hair. When he has completed this highly meticulous activity he puts the comb away and enjoys another moment's contemplation. He spits on the floor, rubs the spit into the ground with his foot and then cracks his knuckles. All these actions are executed with the greatest attention to detail and are outrageously heightened as indicated above. Once* JUDD *has finished his sequence,* RALPH *moves centre stage and repeats the ritual. Once finished, he stands by* JUDD. LES *joins them once more enacting the ritual. Finally they speak. Each word is delivered with much more emphasis than would appear necessary as they acknowledge each other.*)

LES   Judd?

JUDD   Les.

RALPH   Les?

LES   Ralph.

RALPH   Judd?

JUDD   Ralph.

           (LUCKY ERIC *joins the group.*)

ERIC   Ralph?

RALPH   Lucky Eric.

JUDD   Eric?

ERIC   Judd, Les.

LES   Lucky Eric. Alright?

ERIC   Yeah. Why?

LES   Cold innit?

RALPH   Yeh. Bitter.

JUDD   Any trouble last night?

LES   Usual. Couple of punks got glassed.

JUDD   Nothing special then?

RALPH   No.

LES   I wanted to have 'em, but Eric said no.

ERIC   You're too violent, Les. You can't control yourself.

LES   You don't have any fun, Eric. That's your trouble.
Gerrin' past it.

ERIC   (*totally manic*) Don't you ever say that I am getting
past it! Ever!

JUDD   Many in?

RALPH   Packed. Early rush, then it'll tail off.

ERIC   That's Fridays for you.

JUDD   I got a basket meal for nothing yesterday.

ERIC   When?

JUDD   Yesterday.

LES   Who gave it to you?

JUDD   That girl.

ERIC   Oh yeah?

RALPH   Nice one she is, nice tea bag.

JUDD   Not bad.

ERIC   Yeah, alright in the dark.

RALPH   A bit fat around the buttocks if you ask me.

ERIC   Sommat to grab innit?

JUDD   Chicken it was. Tender.

LES   And chips?

JUDD   No chips. Fattening!

ERIC   Short legs.

RALPH   Yeah right.

ERIC   Optical illusion, that is.

JUDD   What? That chips are fattening?

RALPH   How come?

Eric	Makes her arse look bigger.
Les	Nearer to the ground.
Ralph	Good centre of gravity, chickens.
Eric	How's the judo?
Ralph	Not bad, thanks.
Eric	Still training?
Ralph	Yeah, twice a week. And you?
Judd	Couldn't train hamsters.
Eric	I trained you though, didn't I? Everyday, powerlifting. I benchpressed three hundred and fifty-four pounds yesterday.
Les	Who?
Eric	Me.
Les	When?
Eric	Yesterday.
Les	Get pillocked!
Eric	No pillock Thomas. No pillock.
Judd	I've seen him do it.
Les	Yeah?
Eric	Could have done two raps.
Judd	Three hundred and fifty-four pounds, that's, er, twenty…
Ralph	That's heavy, Judd.
Eric	What can you bench, Judd?
Judd	Something.
Eric	Still wrestling?
Judd	No.
Les	Still on the dole are you?
Judd	No.
Ralph	Doing a bit of nicking?

JUDD	No. Well a bit...I'm doing a bit of rugby league...Sunday league stuff...I've started training for it.
ERIC	It's a bit quiet out here tonight, isn't it...too quiet.
RALPH	It'll soon liven up when the pubs turn out. They'll all be streaming down here, like sheep.
ALL	(*chanting*) Here we go, here we go, here we go. (*as if downing another pint.*) FOURTEEN!!
RALPH	Bastards!
ERIC	What time is it?
JUDD	Well, the big hand is on nine...
LES	Early doors yet. No need to start gerrin' aggressive.
RALPH	Yes, they'll all be coming down here, looking for a woman.
LES	Yeah, a big buxom woman.
JUDD	Or a small petite woman.
ERIC	Or a bloke.
JUDD	Yes, there's usually one or two of them about and all.
ERIC	Is there?
LES	They're alright you know really.
RALPH	No, they are not alright you know really.
LES	They are...they are the same as us. They've got the same feelings, the same sex drives.
ERIC	Have they, Leslie?
LES	Yes they have, 'cos one of my best mates...
RALPH	Hold on a minute, Les.
ERIC	What are you on about Les?
LES	Now listen. I was just about to say...
RALPH	Yes...
LES	That one of my best mates...
RALPH	Yes...

LES	Once knew a fella who once and only once, worked in a club for gay people.
ERIC	Tell us another one.
ERIC	You can't be too careful these days, Les.
RALPH	Each to their own. That's it. Each to their bloody own. You have just got to let people get on with what they want...that is my philosophy for life.
ERIC	Fair enough Ralph. Fair enough. I like to hear a man express his philosophy. Fair enough. (*Pause.*) You can borrow my handbag any night, sweetie.
RALPH	Steady on.
ERIC	Yeah?
RALPH	Steady on.
ERIC	Or what?
RALPH	Are we trying to start something, Eric?
ERIC	Could be.
RALPH	Are we trying to encourage a conflict situation?
ERIC	Might be, Mr Inner Calm.

(RALPH *takes up a strong stance and invites* ERIC *to hit him.*)

RALPH	Come on then...there...now...

(ERIC *makes a move as if to hit him, but stops. It is a hoax.* ERIC *stands and laughs at* RALPH. *The other bouncers see the latent danger but as this is a regular occurence, they are not unduly disturbed.*)

RALPH	Powerlifters. I've shit 'em.
ERIC	Judo. Puffballs.

(*They back off. There is a moment's quiet.*)

JUDD	Eric, Eric...Remember that Rugby Union trip that came down.
LES	Zulu warriors?
RALPH	None of that tonight, I hope.

JUDD	Caused chaos.
ERIC	Bloody idiots.
LES	College boys.
ALL	(*sing*) She's a rag shag-a-bag, she's an automatic whore.
JUDD	Chuff heads.
RALPH	College, my arse.
LES	They came down here doing their college antics, hitting each other over the head with beer trays, dropping their trousers every five minutes.
JUDD	Like I said, one or two of them about.
LES	Justin.
JUDD	Rupert.
ERIC	Chaps.
RALPH	Beer races, Zulu warriors. It was like bloody bonanza down here by the time they'd finished. Chairs all over the bloody place. We had to call the cops; let them deal with the maniacs.
ALL	(*chanting in an upper-class accent*) Jolly boating weather, fa la la la la...
RALPH	Supposed to be bleeding educated.
LES	And then one of these awful pickets threw a stone at the policemen's horsey.
ERIC	No.
LES	Yes.
RALPH	Animals to a man. Style, no style. (*Indicating himself.*) Style. And they thought it was funny. I remember talking to one of them.
	(JUDD, ERIC *and* LES *become the students.* RALPH *has to deal with them.* JUDD *stands on a beer barrel. The students are preparing for a beer race.*)
	(*They line up to perform the beer race.*)
ERIC	Here we go, Justin. Beer race. Une, deux, trois.

Les	My go…

(ERIC *and* LES *drink and pour beer over their heads.*)

Les	Now your turn, Justin…oh, he's fluffed it. Get them down, Justin.

(JUDD [JUSTIN] *has fluffed the exercise and consequently has to take his trousers down to the Zulu warrior song.*)

ERIC LES	} Get them down, you Zulu warrior, get them down, you Zulu chief…

(RALPH *approaches to sort them out.*)

RALPH	Oy!
JUDD	What, my good man?
RALPH	Leave it out.
JUDD	Leave what out?
RALPH	You know what I mean, just leave it out.
JUDD	Relax, friend, we are only having a bit of a laugh.
RALPH	It's not funny.
JUDD	Relax.
RALPH	Don't do it.
ALL	(*sing*) When you want to go to it…
RALPH	I said it's not funny. Now you and your mates can just get out.
JUDD	Excuse me, sir, but are you addressing me?
RALPH	Yes.
JUDD	I object to your tone.
ERIC	Ditto.
LES	Ditto.
RALPH	Where are you from?
JUDD	St Lukes.
ALL	Ra!
RALPH	St Lukes what?
ALL	Ra!

JUDD	Christ, mate, we're a college. St Luke's.
ALL	Ra!!
JUDD	We're on a rugby tour. Been playing Cheltenham.
LES	Ra!
JUDD	Not Ra. Rotters.
LES	Oh sorry. Rotters, rotters.
JUDD	You know what it's like, get a stinking skinful piss in a bucket and try and get one of the drunken chaps to drink it.
LES	Well done, rotters.
RALPH	I think that you've had enough, don't you? Come on, out you go.
JUDD	Don't touch me...
RALPH	Look, don't start it...
JUDD	Don't touch me or there'll be a bloody riot in here tonight.
	(RALPH *hits the student. We come out of the scene and he addresses the bouncers.*)
RALPH	I couldn't help it. He was just provoking me, so I let him have one. A hip throw. That's what started it.
LES	Animals.
JUDD	They have these special nights, you know. Rugby clubs. Sex and all that; live.
LES	Yeah?
JUDD	I thought of joining.
ERIC	I was just thinking.
JUDD	What with?
ERIC	My brain, Judd, up here. Where you keep budgie food and dubbin. I've got a brain.
JUDD	You ought to be on Mastermind, Eric, if you've got a brain. Fancy having a brain and doing this job. At this rate you're going to end up on *Krypton Factor* or sommat.

ERIC   And at this rate you're going to end up on a life
        support, Judd.

LES   Leave it out, Eric.

RALPH   You're very tetchy, Eric.

ERIC   Oh yeah?

RALPH   Yes. You're very very tetchy.

LES   What were you thinking about, Eric, with this brain
        that you've got?

ERIC   I was just thinking: women.

LES   Oh yeah, and what about them?

ERIC   They're weird!

LES   They're not as weird as having a beard up your arse.

RALPH   What on earth are you trying to say, Eric?

ERIC   Different attractions. Strange.

JUDD   What's strange about women?

ERIC   They laugh at you when you're naked.

RALPH   I was just thinking as well. I mean, where is
        everybody? I'm freezing to bloody death out here.
        Why's that?

JUDD   Because it's cold.

RALPH   Because nobody's turned up yet, so let me get me
        hands on somebody, warm them up a bit.

JUDD   They'll all be gerrin' some beer down their bloody
        necks, stood about in plush pubs, slopping beer down
        'em. Either that or they're watching the bloody telly,
        come down here about half eleven, tight-fisted sods.

LES   It's still early.

RALPH   I'm going inside in a minute.

        (ERIC *has been gazing into the night.*)

ERIC   Look at them lights, look at all those lights.

JUDD   "The City by night", by Lucky Eric; "an artist's
        impression".

LES	Piss artist.
ERIC	Them lights are like people, just like people's lives.
LES	What's he on about?
ERIC	Them flats, people live in them flats.
JUDD	He's a bloody genius, you know.
ERIC	Couples, huddled together in one or two rooms.
RALPH	Mom, he's nicked me Meccano.
LES	Shut up.
ERIC	Carrying out relationships.
JUDD	Aye aye, here we go. Getting round to sex.
ALL	NO NO NO...YES!
ERIC	In them flats, somebody'll be having a shag right now.

(Pause, while the idea sinks in.)

LES	Lucky bastards...
ERIC	All over the world people will be dying, and conceiving children and growing vegetables and shagging.
LES	Lucky bastards.
RALPH	Don't let it get to you, Eric.
LES	Don't get depressed.
ERIC	And we're stood here out in the cold like four daft pricks.

LES
RALPH } *(shouting)* Lucky Eric's first
JUDD   speech!!

(The three bouncers fade into the background as the lights dim and a spotlight comes up on ERIC. He delivers his speech with total sincerity.)

ERIC   The girls are young; some look younger than the others. It worries me. It does. I'm not thick. You think that we're thick. We're not. *I'm not.* Got to be eighteen. I turn a blind eye. We live by rules but we all turn blind eyes. I don't know whether or not it's a

good thing...still at school half of them; they come
down here Friday, Saturday, saving up all week the
money they've earned working part-time in the
supermarket. What else is there? With their made-up
faces, floating about on a cloud of *Ester Lauder*,
wearing *Impulse* and footless tights, or flashing
wrinkle-free flesh, of schoolgirl knicker dreams, flesh
of sunburnt leg; hairless leg, shapely, untouched by
human hand, leg. I sweat a lot. Wouldn't you? Two
drinks and they're going; legs opening to any
particular denizen of the night with car keys and
Aramis splashed face, maybe even *Old Spice*; Drunken,
free, giddy, silly girls, wanting to be women, done too
soon. Vulnerable, cruel world the morning after, or
the month after when the curse hasn't taken its spell!
I wanna touch them, squeeze them, keep them safe.
Smell like Pomander, a lingering smell. Pure and
dirty, innocent and vulgar; it all withers, washes
away. Eighteen going on thirty-five, because they
think they've got to, because they're forced to...I
dunno.

(*Lights come up and the other bouncers take up their positions
and start to talk once more—all as if the speech had never
occurred.*)

JUDD   Ever have any strange sex, Leslie?

LES   No. Never.

RALPH   I have. I've had some of that.

LES   Yeah? What was it like?

RALPH   Strange.

ERIC   I nearly had chinky once.

JUDD   Oh yeah. Army, was it?

ALL   Shun...

RALPH   In Malaya, was it?

          (*They all make Malaya noises.*)

ERIC   No...Fish and chip shop down Blenheim Terrace.
          Nice woman; didn't understand a word she said
          though.

LES   That the language of love, Eric?

JUDD   Number 34 with rice, eh?

RALPH   Sixty-nine, knowing Lucky Eric.

           (*They all laugh manically.*)

ERIC   Couldn't go through with it.

JUDD   Why?

ERIC   Married.

LES   He's crazy.

JUDD   I'm in the mood tonight.

RALPH   Tell us something new.

JUDD   I could shag a rat.

RALPH   The power of the spoken word.

           (*Lighting suddenly changes and loud music booms. We are
           transported into the nightclub.* RALPH *plays the DJ.*)

RALPH   Hope that you're all having a greeeaaat time down
           here at *Mr Cinders*. Remember that on Tuesday, yes
           that's Tuesday of next week, we'll be having a video
           special. So do come along and enjoy that
           extravaganza. I shall be giving away a few bottles of
           champagne very shortly for a number of people who
           are celebrating their twenty-first today; key of the
           door and, lets hope, key of another special place. Are
           there any nymphomaniacs down here this evening?
           Yes, there are. Well, I'll be playing something for you
           very soon, and it will not be a record. Okay, okay,
           let's just stop the music for a moment, and put up
           your hand, yes put up your hand if you are a virgin.
           I don't believe it, ladies and gentlemen, there are no
           virgins down here this evening. Looks like it's going
           to be a night to remember. This is Shalamar...

           (*The music plays loudly. The four actors now become*
           ELAINE, ROSIE, SUZY *and* MAUREEN. *They pick up their
           handbags and walk with great dignity into the middle of the
           dance floor. They then all place their handbags in a pile on the
           floor and begin to dance around the bags to the music.*)

ALL	(*with the song*) 'When you love someone, it's natural not demanding...'
ERIC	Maureen—short but nice, fat but sickly.
LES	Rosie—feels a bit tiddly.
JUDD	Elaine—sweating like a race horse, wants to sit down.
RALPH	Suzy—sexy and flashing it about a bit.
JUDD	Christ, I'm sweating.
LES	Ya what?
JUDD	I'm dripping.
RALPH	I am.
ERIC	I feel sick...
RALPH	You what?
ERIC	I feel sick.
LES	It's too warm.
JUDD	Ya what Rosie?
LES	I feel dizzy.
JUDD RALPH }	Happy Birthday.
LES	Shut up.
ERIC	I think I'm gonna spew.
JUDD	Oh isn't she pathetic?
ERIC	Let me get to the toilet.
LES	What's she had?
RALPH	Five barley wines.
ERIC	Hang on a minute. I feel alright now, it was just indigestion.
JUDD	(*to the audience*) And then, as if by magic, the drunken tears, and Rosie discovers twenty-firsts are not all fun...
ERIC	Her boyfriend Patrick is seen kissing another...

RALPH   With several large shorts imbibed, the tears and mascara begin to run.

LES   He's left me for another, over in a dark corner snogging, and French kissing, tongue job to say the least. I feel myself get all angry and upset inside but I've already had enough drinks to fill a bath. The hate turns inside to self-pity and the tears begin to flow and with it the mascara. And soon my face looks like a miner's back in the showers, rivulets of black *Max Factor*. And then the friends...

ALL   That's us.

LES   ...begin to comfort me and offer me advice on how and what to do.

JUDD   Burn her face off.

LES   Oh don't be daft, Elaine.

ERIC   Castrate the philanderer.

RALPH   Finish with him.

LES   Then the plague begins to spread, the tears begin to flow and all advice becomes sobbing woe. Look at him sitting there as cool as a cucumber. I've been going out with him for two days...it's pathetic.

ALL   Pathetic, pathetic, pathetic...

         (*Loud music comes up.*)

RALPH   I love this. I've gorra dance.

ERIC   Oooooooh, it goes right through me.

RALPH   It goes right through me an' all.

LES   What hasn't?

RALPH   I heard that, Rosie.

LES   I'm sorry, Sue.

ALL   (*with song*) Ooh wee...

         (*Lights change and we are suddenly outside the club once more.* ERIC *and* JUDD *are the two bouncers, patrolling the doors.* RALPH *and* LES *play a variety of characters trying to enter the club.*)

ERIC	Seems to be going quite steady.
JUDD	Yeah. Look out, a couple of young lads here.
	(RALPH and LES *appear on the scene.*)
RALPH	Jock.
LES	And Birdy...all dressed up, very smart.
RALPH	But we look a bit rough.
BOTH	Hey, come ed, come ed.
LES	Hey!
RALPH	What?
LES	Brookside, yeah.
RALPH	Hey!
LES	What?
RALPH	Bleasdale, yeah.
LES	Hey!
RALPH	What?
LES	Beatles, yeah.
BOTH	Yeah yeah yeah!
ERIC	Evening fellas.
BOTH	Evening.
JUDD	Where you from?
LES	About.
JUDD	Oh yeah?
ERIC	Not from round about here, are you?
RALPH	No, not round about here.
ERIC	Oh.
LES	Is there a problem?
JUDD	No, no problem.
LES	Great we're in, come on.
ERIC	Are you out sort of celebrating like?

RALPH	Yeah, you could say that.
LES	Yeah, we're celebrating, yeah.
ERIC	What, a stag night is it, lads?
LES	Yeah that's right, a stag night.
JUDD	Sorry lads, can't let you in.
RALPH	Why?
ERIC	No stag night parties allowed in.
LES	You what?
ERIC	You heard.
RALPH	Jesus Christ.
JUDD	Sorry fellas, but rules is rules.
RALPH } LES }	Please.
ERIC	Go away.
RALPH } LES }	Come ed, come ed, come ed.
	(*They go off.*)
ERIC	Soft bastards.
JUDD	Always works.
ERIC	Stag nights; it's always a good laugh.
JUDD	No wonder they're losing custom in here.
	(RALPH *and* LES *now become* MARK *and* BRIAN.)
RALPH	Mark—drives a Mini, car keys in hand, open-neck shirt, even in winter.
LES	Brian—very cool, did some karate, thinks he's Bruce Lee. More tea Mr Prize Fight?
RALPH	No thanks Mr Lee.
LES	Evening.
JUDD	Evening.
RALPH	Evening...waiter.

LES	What a marvellous joke.
RALPH	I know, and it just sort of came to me.
JUDD	Where are ya going?
LES	In there my good man.
JUDD	Oh yeah?
RALPH	Yeah
JUDD	You're not.
LES	Why?
JUDD	Look, don't get clever, sunbeam.
LES	*Look*??
JUDD	Listen bastard, do you want dropping?
LES	Come on then, let's go down to *Tiffs*…
RALPH	Under the circumstances, a rather good idea. Taxi. (*They exit.*)
ERIC	(*with mounting laughter*) *Tiffs*…*Tiffs*…*Tiffs*… It's shut!
JUDD	(*laughing*) Shut!
	(RALPH and LES *enter again, this time as punks. They spread their hands above their heads to create spikey hair, spit, spew, pogo, etc.*)
JUDD	Where are you punks going?
LES	In the discotheque, man.
ERIC	Not dressed like that you're not. Go home and change your tutu.
RALPH	Hey man don't mess with my tutu.
ERIC	Don't call me man …forkhead.
RALPH	Come on man, we're not going to cause any trouble in there. (*He spits.*)
JUDD	I know you're not 'cos I'm not going to let you in. (*He spits on Ralph.*)
RALPH	Hey did you see that?

Les	Yes I did, and I think it was a very good shot...come on, let's go and have a pint of piss in the cesspit...
Ralph	Hey Ruffage.
Les	Yes Ashley.
Ralph	DO you know what they are?...they are fascist pigs...they've spoilt the whole evening and I am shortly intending to write a song about the experience.
Les	Go on then.
Ralph	Fascist pigs.
Les	Fascist pigs.
Ralph	(*singing*) Oh you fascist pigs...
Les	(*singing*) Oh you fascist pigs...
Ralph	What do think of that then?
Les	They're lovely lyrics.

(LES *and* RALPH *pogo off upstage. The actors suddenly change position so that* ERIC *and* JUDD *become the lads,* TERRY *and* BAZ, *and* RALPH *and* LES *become bouncers once more.*)

Eric Judd	(*chanting*) Here we go, here we go, here we go...
Eric	Watch these two, Terry.
Judd	Why's that, Baz?
Eric	Might be a bit awkward.
Ralph	Evening, lads.
Eric	Evening.
Les	Are you members?
Judd	You what?
Ralph	Members only tonight, lads, sorry.
Judd	It wasn't members only last night.
Eric	Or last Friday. Play the game, fellas.

RALPH	Only pillocking, lads. In you come. Thirty-eight quid each.
JUDD	You what? Hear that, Baz?
ERIC	It's only thirty bob.
LES	Let them in, Ralph.
RALPH	In you come...

(ERIC *and* JUDD *enter the club, and walk upstage.*)

RALPH	Why did you let them in?
LES	I'm going to do that fat one.
RALPH	You're weird, Les.
LES	Oh yeah.
RALPH	With the greatest respect you're very weird.
LES	I know.

(*They all now become the lads.*)

ERIC	Baz—
JUDD	Terry—
RALPH	Jerry—
LES	Kev—

(*They all take another imaginary pint and slop it down.*)

ALL	SIXTEEN!! And a vindaloo!
LES	In the toilets—
ERIC	Lav—
RALPH	Bog—
JUDD	Shit house—

(*Standing upstage centre, they are in the club toilets. Each of them passes wind and there is a delight of visual scatalogical jokes. Finally, they are ready to urinate.* LES *narrates, conveying the atmosphere whilst the others act out the situation.*)

LES	At about twelve o'clock, the toilets are the hell-hole of the disco.

ALL	Scenes from Dante's *Inferno!!*
LES	Keeping your feet on the slippery tiled floor is a feat in itself. Many an aff-air has been ruined by loose footing; one quick slip and you're up to your hip in urine...

(One of the actors slips and drowns.)

LES	When you actually reach the urinals, your Hush Puppies are soaking, seeping through to your socks. In the urinals, there is by this time a liberal smattering of tab ends, and the odd soupçon of sick. In the sink there's probably a durex packet, with the condoms still inside, some forgetful stud having left them.
LES	The smell is nauseous; you stand holding your breath trying to pee, reading the wall, trying your best not to catch anyone's eye.
ERIC	*(reading)* You don't come here to mess about so have a piss and...oh, charming...
JUDD	*(reading)* Follow this line... *(he follows a line, moving slowly)* You are now pissing on your foot.
ERIC	Rearrange this well-known phrase. Shit Mrs Thatcher is a...
RALPH	I've got it! Mrs Shit is a Thatcher.
JUDD	Don't be stupid. It's...Shit Thatcher, Mrs is a...
LES	Here's one; save water, piss on a friend.

(They start to look at one anothers' genitals.)

ERIC	*(to RALPH)* What the hell is that?
RALPH	It's mine.
ERIC	Jesus Christ!
JUDD	What's up?
ERIC	Look at that.
JUDD	Bloody hell.
RALPH	What's the matter with you lot?
ERIC	*(to LES)* Hey, seen this?

LES	What?
ERIC	Look at that, I've never seen one so big.
LES	Bleeding hell…
RALPH	Haven't you seen one before?
ERIC	It's like a baby's arm with an orange in its fist.
RALPH	Let's have a look at yours then.
ERIC	Gerra way, you pervert.
JUDD	It's not natural.
LES	It is an offensive weapon. He could mug somebody with it.
RALPH	Oh yeah.
LES	Come on, let's get back on the dance floor.
ERIC	Do you fancy a bit of a laugh?
ALL	Yeah… (*laughter.*)
	(*They become bouncers once more.*)
ERIC	Ralph get the kettle on… Les get the chocolate biscuits out…
JUDD	Why?
ERIC	It's the interval.

INTERVAL

RALPH, JUDD *and* LES *enter and form a line, centre stage.* LUCKY ERIC *joins the line, inspecting the audience.*

JUDD	(*to audience*) What are you laughing at?
ERIC	Do you think they're ready for it?
LES	No. But they're gonna get it.
	(*Loud disco music plays.* RALPH *becomes the DJ once again. The others become the lads, by now fairly drunk, attempting to dance whilst the DJ speaks.*)

RALPH   Yeah! Wow! Things are really happening down here
        tonight. Have some fun, yeah have some fun. Tell
        you what girls...tell you what we'll do...the first girl
        who brings me a matching pair of bra and knickers,
        yes a pair of knickers and a bra, there'll be a bottle of
        Asti Spumante and a fortnight's free entry, get it,
        entry, to *Mr Cinders*. So come on girls, get them off
        and bring them up to me, marvellous Michael Dee,
        the DJ with the big B...

        (ERIC *plays a very drunk heavy metal freak. He approaches
        the DJ.*)

ERIC   Hey!

RALPH   I don't care what size they are, girls, as long as they
        are clean.

ERIC   Hey man!

RALPH   Yeah.

ERIC   Hey man!

RALPH   What's the problem, man?

ERIC   Play sommat decent.

RALPH   This is decent.

ERIC   Play sommat decent.

RALPH   Go away, man. Get it together.

ERIC   It's rubbish.

RALPH   Everybody's gerrin' off on it man, you know. I mean
        what're you saying? You're talking crap.

ERIC   It's shit.

RALPH   Well that may be your opinion but every one seems to
        be enjoying it.

ERIC   Hey man, ya got any Deep Purple?

RALPH   (*over the microphone.*) Bouncers to the DJ...bouncers to
        the DJ...

ERIC   Hey man, have you got any Yes?

RALPH   Who?

ERIC	Hey, they'll do man. I saw them at Knebworth. They've got a better stack than this tinny shit…how many watts have you got, man…hey get off me…

(*LES and* JUDD *appear as bouncers, ready to cart him off.*)

JUDD	Come on.
ERIC	Tell him to put something decent on.
JUDD	Take it steady, pal.
ERIC	Do you like Status Quo?
JUDD	No, but I like Perry Como. Now get out.

(*The bouncers throw him out of the club. All four now become bouncers again. They are back on the door. It is growing late. They begin to sigh heavily, looking down the road to see if any one is coming. By now they are bored and cold.*)

RALPH	I think that the snot up my nose is frozen.
ERIC	Very interesting.
RALPH	Aren't you cold?
ERIC	No, I've got blood in my veins, not water.
JUDD	All fat, that's why.
ERIC	Listen what's talking.
JUDD	That's muscle.
ERIC	That's shit.
RALPH	That's enough.
ERIC	Roll on two o'clock.
JUDD	Have we got any films in?
LES	Yeah. A bluey; it'll make your nose run, it's that blue.
JUDD	Where did you get it?
ALL	Video shop.

(*Scene change to the video shop.* ERIC *and* RALPH *are looking for videos.* JUDD *plays the shop assistant.*)

LES	Have you got any of them video nasties?

JUDD   No, no, no, no...YES.

LES   Oh...what have you got?

JUDD   I've got *Rambo One, Rambo Two, Rambo Three* to
        thirty-seven, *Friday the Thirteenth, Friday the Fifteenth,
        Monday the Twenty-third, October the Ninth, My Mother's
        Birthday, Bank Holiday Sunday* and most of the
        Religious Holidays in Three D.

RALPH   *Queen Kong*, the story of a sixty-four foot gay gorilla.

LES   Yes that's it, something a bit blue.

JUDD   I've got light blue, dark blue, sky blue, and navy
        blue.

LES   Navy blue?

JUDD   Or something with animals...

        (*They all grunt and gurgle like animals.*)

LES   I'll take the one with animals. The boys should enjoy
        this.

        (*Back outside the club.*)

ERIC   Perverts...

JUDD   At two o'clock the disco shuts...free drinks all round.

LES   At least we've got a video now.

RALPH   Yeah, you can say that again.

LES   At least we've got a video now.

JUDD   Which beats the old projector we used to have...three-
        quarters of an hour fixing up the bloody projector.
        Then with sweaty hand in tight polyster, we'd watch
        the twitchin' and the screamin'. Like fish in a barrel,
        we'd fidget and jump watching plot and orifice
        explored.

        (*All the bouncers have a drink. They then mime setting up the
        projector, ready to watch the blue movie.* RALPH *and* ERIC
        act out the film. ERIC *plays a buxom Swede taking her clothes
        off, about to have a shower.* RALPH *plays the postman.
        Sleazy background music and strobe lights should give the scene
        a cinematic feel. The other bouncers provide a commentary.*)

RALPH	(*as though the doorbell*) Bing bong...
ERIC	Whom de iz eet?
RALPH	It ist me. Nobby, ze Swedish postmant...
LES	Hey up. It's Nobby, Swedish postman.
ERIC	Come on ze in, Nobby. I'm unt der shopwer, unt...
LES	(*excitedly*) Go on, Nobby lad...
RALPH	Ver ist der usband?
ERIC	Engagedist unt ont dert buziness...
LES	Husband away on business...
JUDD	Go on, Nob!
ERIC	I am zo lonely wit my usband in Oslo...
LES	Aye, aye...she's lonely with her husband away on business in Oslo. I can understand that. Can you Judd? A woman alone and all that.
JUDD	Gerron with the film.
ERIC	Oh, I've dropped the soapen on the flooren.
RALPH	She's dropped the soapen on the flooren.
LES	She's dropped the soap.
JUDD	Go on...Nobby, my son...

(As NOBBY [Eric] *is about to move the action freezes as if the film has jammed. Strobe stops.*)

JUDD	Give that projector a boot.
ALL	Boot!

(*Strobe re-starts. The action is now played in reverse, as though the film is being rewound, up to the doorbell ringing at the start. We snap out of this scene and the actors are all bouncers again.*)

JUDD	It's not fair.
ERIC	Porno films...a waste of time.
JUDD	It pays your wages.
LES	There's something wrong with a bloke who doesn't enjoy a good bluey, that's what I say.

RALPH	I think that's a fair comment, Les.
JUDD	Eric doesn't like them. He thinks its degrading.
LES	What's degrading about it; they get paid for it. I mean its not exactly as if they're doing it for peanuts.
JUDD	I'd do it for peanuts. I'd do it for nothing. What a job? Eh? What a job? It's not exactly a matter of being a good actor is it? Just get in there, get stripped off, get stuck in…Not a bad job Eric, eh? Beats this shit.
ERIC	You're an animal, Judd.
JUDD	Keep talking…
ERIC	An animal…
JUDD	How's that?
ERIC	Don't you know?
ALL	(*very softly*) Lucky Eric's second speech.

(*As* ERIC *speaks, the others can act out the scene. Background music should play.*)

ERIC   I'm sat in this pub, just an ordinary pub, and it's Christmas. Everybody's had one over the eight. And there's a group of lads, football supporters, that type, Eleven stone walking about like they think they're Frank Bruno: And there's this girl nineteen, twenty, and she's drunk, and she's got it all there, the figure, the looks. The lads are laughing, joking with her. "Give us a kiss eh?" and she does. Well, it's Christmas, I think, well, it is Christmas. I sat watching for an hour. She was well pissed; they all had a go, kissing her, feeling her, lifting her skirt up. Nobody noticed, pub was packed. Merry Christmas they'd say, and line up for another kiss and a feel, each one going further than the other, until I could see the tops of her thighs bare. And in that pub, she had them all, or they had her, six of 'em, in a pub. Nobody noticed, nobody noticed but me. It was a strange feeling, a weird feeling, I remember walking over to where they were. I was aroused more than ever before in my life. I'm so powerful, so powerful. I stood in front of them, looking at them. The first head was quite hard, but the others were soft, like eggs; they hit the wall and smashed. The girl stood up. "Give us a kiss", she said, "give us a kiss." "Go home", I said, "please go home…"

(*Lights come up.*)

LES   So what's the plan then?

JUDD   Inside?

LES   Yeah.

RALPH   The usual.

LES   What if there's a big fight, rush in, eh? Get some kicks in.

ERIC   Don't be a twat all your life, Les, have a night off.

LES   A few kicks never hurt anybody.

JUDD   Look at all those lights…them lights are like people…they are like people's lights…

ERIC   Anybody could do this job.

LES   Bollocks!

ERIC   No they could, it's a matter of ego.

LES   Isn't that Frankenstein's mate?

RALPH   That's Igor.

LES   Same innit?

ERIC   His brain's—painted on.

LES   But he's handy though, Eric.

ERIC   I'm telling you. It's all image.

RALPH   Eric's got a point. I once heard some talk of a nightclub in Manchester that employed a woman.

JUDD   Bollocks…

LES   Pull the other one…

RALPH   Straight up is this; she was a big fat woman.

JUDD   I know her.

RALPH	Whenever somebody was making an arsehole of themselves, she'd go over and tell 'em not to be so stupid, tell them to pull themselves together. She never had any trouble either.
JUDD	Can't see that happening down here; she'll probably get glassed.
LES	Or picked up.
ALL	HA HA HA

(*Inside the disco.* RALPH *becomes* SUZY, ERIC *becomes* BAZ, LES *becomes* KEV *and* JUDD *becomes* ELAINE.)

ERIC	It's ten past one. Baz is well gone.
LES	Kev is ready to try it on, with anyone with two legs and two tits. Two teeth, anything.
JUDD	Plain Elaine has got a pain in her head, she's ready for bed.
RALPH	Suzy is sexy, she's been flirting about.
ERIC	What about those two? Come on let's get in, have a bash.
LES	Just gimme a sec. I'm dying for a slash.

(LES *moves off.* ERIC [BAZ] *now walks up to the girls.*)

ERIC	Now then girls, alright are we?
JUDD	Piss off fatty.
ERIC	You can't get around me that easy.
JUDD	You're ugly.
ERIC	That's nice…What's your name?
RALPH	Suzy. I'm drunk you know?
ERIC	Wanna have a dance?
RALPH	What about my friend?
ERIC	I've got a mate, he's just gone for a slash, he'll be back in a dash. Come on shall we go…
JUDD	Hey, I hope I'm not gonna be left here?
RALPH	I'm only going for a dance, Elaine, that's all.

(ERIC *and* RALPH *move upstage as if to the dance floor and freeze.* LES *comes back from the toilet, and is faced with* JUDD [ELAINE].)

LES   Where's Baz?

JUDD   Is he fat?

LES   A bit.

JUDD   He's just got off with my friend.

LES   The lucky gett! Go on, pole it. He always gets the pretty ones.

JUDD   D'you wanna dance?

LES   Who me?

JUDD   Come on, I like you.

LES   Gerroff me.

(*Both couples now take up a smooching position. They begin to think aloud.*)

ERIC   God! She smells great, her chest's really warm. I can just about feel her arse. I think she's drunk. Oh no, I'm gerrin' a hard on. She's rubbin' herself against me. (ERIC *moves his body in order to dance away from* RALPH [SUZY].)

RALPH   I don't know where I am, I'm sinking and spinning, round and round, round and round...

JUDD   So am I.

LES   This is bad news, I hope nobody sees me. I think Terry's drunk anyway. She's strong is this one. She's breaking my bleeding back. I just hope that she doesn't fall over. I can feel her fat.

JUDD   If he makes a move or tries anything with me I'll break his arms. He's nice and cute though, I'll say that much. I think he likes me...

LES   She is the ugliest girl I've ever met...

ERIC   I think I've pulled a cracker this time...

RALPH   I'll let him take me home but I'm not having sex.

ERIC	I bet she goes like a rabbit.
LES	I hope she doesn't try and kiss me. I'll spew.
ERIC	Wait while I tell all the lads.
RALPH	His breath smells awful, I think he must smoke.
ERIC	Yes, I'm in here, no trouble.
RALPH	He's really too big, a bit of a joke. He's not what I'm after, not handsome and slim. I'll tell him I'm going to the loo, that should lose him...I'll have to nip to the toilet.
ERIC	You what?
RALPH	I've got to go to the toilet.
ERIC	What for?
RALPH	Don't be nosey.
ERIC	Don't be long, will yer?
RALPH	You wait here, don't move. I'll be back in a tick.
ERIC	Right.
	(RALPH *walks away from* ERIC. ERIC *freezes as he looks at his watch.*)
LES	Listen.
JUDD	What?
LES	I'll have to go now.
JUDD	Why?
LES	I should have turned into a pumpkin ten minutes ago.
JUDD	Oh yeah.
LES	Look can you let me go please...
JUDD	Give me a kiss first...
LES	I can't.
JUDD	Why?
LES	I've got something that I don't want you to catch.
JUDD	What's that?

LES	Me. I've got a terminal disease.
JUDD	You haven't, you're only saying that.
LES	Like fuck I am!!
JUDD	You're stopping here with me or I'll chop your face off...
LES	Oh Christ...get off, you old bag.
ALL	(*shout*) FIGHT!!

(*They all now dash to the centre of the stage, as bouncers and lads, grab each other and generally give the impression that there is a fight going on.*)

ERIC	Come on you two. Leave it out. Get them out, Judd. Fire exit.
JUDD	Let's do the bastards.
ERIC	Let's just get them out.
JUDD	I'm going to do mine.
ERIC	Don't.
JUDD	Who are you talking to Eric?
ERIC	You, you daft bastard.
JUDD	Oh yeah.
RALPH	Hey no need to fight over us lads.
ERIC	Piss off... There's no need to do them over, just leave them. They're pissed up anyway.
JUDD	Who do you think you are, Eric?
ERIC	Nobody.
JUDD	You get up my back.
ERIC	Look, Judd, don't set me off.
JUDD	You weird bastard!
LES	How weird?
ERIC	I said, don't set me off.
JUDD	You shouldn't be doing this job. You should be bouncing at *Mothercare*. You're soft.

ERIC   (now quite manic) Don't set me off.

JUDD   Soft inside.

ERIC   Don't set me...

JUDD   Soft bastard...

(*This is now too much for* ERIC *to take; He attacks* JUDD *with a finger.* JUDD *quivers. Suitably violent music comes up as all the bouncers suddenly become psycopaths for a few seconds. They all stop dead.*)

ERIC   Sorry, Judd. Sorry.

ALL   Lucky Eric's third and final speech.

(*A spotlight picks out* ERIC.)

ERIC   Now is the winter of our discontent...may glorious summer...

ALL   Come on Eric...that's enough...

(*Blackout. We return to disco.* RALPH *plays the DJ.*)

RALPH   Someone has just handed me a piece of paper from the dance-floor and on it, it asks me to dedicate this record to Sharon and David, who are out there getting it together. So tell him you love him, Shaz, and tell her you love her, Davs. After all a little white lie never really hurt anyone now did it...but lets be serious for a moment shall we.... All of you girls out there tonight at *Mr. Cinders,* later on when you're really getting it together, spare a thought for me and for our doormen who couldn't even pull a muscle. They'll certainly be going home lonesome tonight...

ERIC   You're dead pal.

RALPH   Just having a joke, Eric...so remember me, marvellous Michael D, your love doctor...

ALL   Jerry—Terry—Kev—Baz—

(*The bouncers become the lads. It is now getting late, they are very drunk, and making efforts to pick up a girl...Five minutes until the club closes.*)

RALPH   I was right, you know?

ERIC	What d'you mean?
RALPH	There are only ugly 'uns left at two o'clock.
ERIC	I had one, but she walked off.
LES	Was she drunk?
JUDD	Must have been.
ERIC	Thanks.
LES	What about them four, over there?
RALPH	You what? She must weigh about seventeen stones.
ERIC	Better than nothing.
LES	She'd eat me.
JUDD	She'd eat us all.
ERIC	What do you say to someone that big?
LES	Sod off. You're big.
JUDD	Sod off ya pig.
OTHERS	No no no. He said big...
JUDD	Sod off ya big pig...it wasn't me that said that, it was me brother... and I haven't even got a brother...
LES	You have, he's in *Star Trek*...You're right you know, there are only scrag ends left at two o'clock.
JUDD	Sod you lot, I'm game.
ALL	And me.
	(*The lads begin to dance with imaginary women.*)
RALPH	Hey you don't sweat much for a big girl do you?
ERIC	Can I borrow your face; I'm going ratting tomorrow?
LES	Do you want a drink? The bar's over there.
JUDD	Give us a kiss, come on....
RALPH	Didn't I used to go to school with you?
LES	Does your dad race pigeons..?
ERIC	Does your shit stink?

ALL   Ooooohhhh.

           (*Slowly the lads change back to the bouncers. It is closing time
           and the bouncers encourage people to leave, see them off, etc.*)

ERIC   Goodnight.

LES   Night love, take care.

JUDD   Goodnight.

RALPH   'Night...

ERIC   Take it nice and steady.

LES   (*Looking at an imaginary woman.*) Look at the arsehole
           on that.

RALPH   She's had a skinful...

JUDD   She's got handles on her hips.

           (LES *becomes a punter, leaving the disco.*)

LES   I've had a great night, fellas... I've had a wonderful
           evening.

ERIC   Come away from him, mate.

LES   Does anyone know where I can get another bottle of
           champagne?

ERIC   You've had enough.

LES   Just one more bottle of champers, and everything will
           be tickety-tickety-boo.

JUDD   Tickety-tickety-fucking-boo.

RALPH   Nut the posh bastard.

JUDD   ...Nut.

LES   Goodnight.

LES   (as a bouncer) Yeah goodnight, sir.

JUDD   Watch this I'll nut him.

ERIC   Goodnight.

RALPH   Have a safe journey home.

           (LES *becomes a bouncer once more.*)

LES   Goodnight. She's down here every night is that one.

JUDD	I thought I'd seen her before.
LES	She's been hanging around me like flies round shit.
ERIC	You said that Les not us...
LES	I think she's after something.
RALPH	'Eat shit five million flies can't be wrong.'
LES	What?
ERIC	Nice to hear that old one again. Goodnight love...
ALL	Goodnight...Goodnight...Goodnight...Goodnight ...Goodnight...

JUDD
ERIC ⎬ (as lads) Here we go, here we go, here we go...
RALPH

(Change of scene to an empty shopping precinct. ERIC becomes the owner of a hot-dog stand. The other bouncers play the lads.)

ERIC   Hot-dogs. Hot-dogs with onions. Beefburgers. Cheeseburgers. With or without onions. Hot-dogs...

(The lads approach the stand.)

ERIC   Right then fellas. What d'you want? Hot-dogs? With or without? Cheeseburger? With or without? Or with red or brown sauce?

LES   Two pints of lager please.

ERIC   Oh, oh, well we have got a little joker here, haven't we?

RALPH   Do you do pizzas?

ERIC   Very funny.

JUDD   I'll have a kebab. Got any kebabs?

ERIC   Yeah. I've got some kebabs.

JUDD   I'll have a kebab.

RALPH   Yeah, and I'll have a kebab.

LES   And me...

JUDD   Three kebabs.

Eric	With onions?
Judd	Yeah. Three with onions.

(Eric *mimes putting sausages into hot-dog rolls.*)

Eric	Three quid, lads.
Judd	Great stuff.
Eric	You want sauce?
Ralph	Quick service, innit?
Les	Yeah.
Eric	You want any sauce?
Judd	Chilli?
Eric	Red or brown?
Ralph	Hey. This ain't a kebab. It's an hot-dog.
Eric	Listen. If I say it's a bleeding kebab then it's a bleeding kebab. Right?
All	Right boss.
Eric	Now sod off !

(*Scene change to the lads now waiting for a taxi.*)

Eric	Baz—
Judd	Terry—
Ralph	Jerry—
Les	Kev—
All	Waaaaaaaaaaay!
Judd	Have you seen the length of this taxi queue? I'm friggin' freezin'.
Les	I wish I'd've put a big coat on.
Ralph	Oh no look at that…I've got spew all over me shoe.
Les	I have.
Judd	I have.
Eric	I've got shit on mine.
All	Waaaaayyyy!

JUDD	Innit dark?
LES	Well it is half-past three.
JUDD	Half-past bloody three and we're stood out in the cold freezin' to bloody death.
ERIC	Just think, *if* I'd've got off with that Suzy I'd be in bed now snuggling up to her brown, tanned sunburnt soft body.
ALL	Whaaaaaaaaaaaaaaay!!!
LES	Innit quiet? All asleep, and tucked away in their little boxes. Innit quiet? Listen, listen to the city. Quiet, innit? All those people asleep; it's like being in a painting.
ERIC	I'm dying for a slash.
RALPH	Do you feel pissed up.
JUDD	Who?
RALPH	You?
JUDD	(*considering the possibility*) No. Not now.
RALPH	No, I don't.
JUDD	I did about an hour ago. I've sobered up. I think.
LES	It's the cold.
ERIC	I'm having a slash. (*He begins to urinate.*)
LES	(*pretending a taxi approaches*) TAXI!
ERIC	Oh shit!! (*He attempts to do up his flys.*)
LES	Only a joke.
JUDD	I've spent thirty-five quid.
RALPH	Yeah?
JUDD	Jesus Christ I've spent thirty-five bleeding quid?
RALPH	I have.
JUDD	That had to last me till Wednesday.
ERIC	Feel better after that slash.
JUDD	Thirty-five quid! I didn't even get a kiss or a feel of tit. Pissing hell, I'm depressed.

RALPH   We all are.

LES   (*to audience*) Another social comment?

JUDD   No, no. Keep it going.

LES   Alright, it's up to you...I've spent forty quid – next
         week's board money. My mam'll have a fit.

ERIC   I've spent...er...I've forgot what I came out with. I've
         only got thirty-seven pence left.

JUDD   Yeah, but thirty-five quid.

RALPH   (*hails a taxi*) Taxi! St John's flats...waaaaaay!

LES   Hey look, it's them four birds!

         (*Whoops of delight as the taxi arrives. They mime getting into
         the taxi and it screeches off. They sit moving as though in a
         car. One of the lads lights a cigarette and begins to smoke.
         One of the others begins to feel sick.*)

RALPH   I feel sick.

         (*The actors convey the sensation that the car is speeding away
         and taking corners at fast speed.* RALPH *begins to retch.*)

RALPH   Tell him to stop.

ERIC   I want another slash.

RALPH   Tell him to stop or I'm gonna be sick.

JUDD   (*as though speaking to the driver*) Will you stop? He says
         he's not stopping 'cos it might be a trick.

ERIC   A trick? What's he want me to do? Rupture my
         bladder?

LES   I feel a bit spewy. Tell him to slow down.

RALPH   Tell him to stop.

JUDD   I've told him.

LES   Let some air in here. It's like a wrestler's jock strap.

         (ERIC *urinates out of the window. It all blows back into the
         others' faces.*)

ERIC   I'm doing it out of the window.

LES   Don't be so bloody stupid.

ERIC	Hey lads, I'm slashing out of the window...
RALPH	Errm...I've been sick down his back.
JUDD	Window...dick...SHUT! (*He shuts the window.*)
ERIC	Aaaargh!!
	(*The car suddenly screeches to a halt.*)
ALL	Home.
	(*Scene switches back to the bouncers at the club.*)
RALPH	Look at the bleeding mess.
ERIC	Animals.
	(JUDD *sings nonsense into the microphone.*)
LES	Look at the amount of beer that's been left. A waste is that, waste.
	(*They stand around contemplating the mess.*)
JUDD	Shall we get packed away and get the video on?
ERIC	Eager tonight Judd, aren't you?
JUDD	I wanna see the filth.
ERIC	You are too sensitive Judd, that's your problem.
RALPH	Look at the mess. Hey there's a pair of knickers over here.
LES	Keep 'em, they might fit you.
JUDD	I'll give you one pound twelve for 'em.
ERIC	Have you seen the bogs?
LES	What's wrong with them?
ERIC	Two urinals cracked, it's all over the floor.
JUDD	What is?
RALPH	(*still rummaging around*) Anybody want a basket meal? One here, still warm.
ERIC	Ah ah...look at this?
LES	What?
ERIC	Another fiver.

JUDD   Jammy bastard.

ERIC   That's four nights on the trot.

RALPH   That's why they call him 'lucky' Eric.

JUDD   Are we gerrin' the video on or what?

ERIC   He is a pervert.

RALPH   Well I don't know about you lads but I'm shagged.

LES   And me.

JUDD   I wish I was.

ERIC   I wish you was and all, Judd.

RALPH   Innit peaceful? Listen how quiet it is.

JUDD   My ears are still buzzing.

ERIC   My brains buzzing. I'm going deaf.

LES   You what?

ERIC   I said...Oh very funny lads; you lads are definitely on the ball at this late hour.

JUDD   Hey, are we gerrin' this chuffin video on or what?

LES   Yeah. Ralph get some cans and we'll have a couple of hours.

LES   Are you stopping Eric?

ERIC   I'm not a pervert.

JUDD   Look what I just found.

ERIC   What?

JUDD   A ten pence piece... Come on... look he's dying to stop.

ERIC   No... I'm gonna get off home.

JUDD   Just watch the first bit.

ERIC   No, I'm not stopping.

RALPH   Come on Eric, spoil yourself.

LES   Yeah, come on.

ERIC   No, I...

JUDD   Come on, man...

ERIC   Well, OK. I'll stop for the first three hours.

JUDD   Right. Where's that video with animals in it? Gerrit
        on!

LES   Alright, Judd.

        (*They put on the imaginary video. It is Michael Jackson's*
        Thriller. *Music comes up and the lights fade to green, as the
        bouncers all don monster's teeth. They proceed to do a
        complicated rip off of the* Thriller *video; moving forwards
        and backwards, grotesquely slouching their shoulders, clapping
        their hands, etc. Note: the* Thriller *video should be carefully
        studied in order to achieve just the right elements of parody.
        Eventually the lights come up and the music stops.*)

        (*The rap music from the start of the play comes up once
        more.*)

ALL   I said a hip hop
        a hippy a hippy
        a hip hip hop and don't you stop

        DOWN AT THE DISCO WAS THE PLACE TO
        BE
        THE LIGHTS WERE SO BRIGHT LIKE A
        COLOUR TV
        THE MUSIC WAS LOUD AND THE BEER
        FLOWED FREE
        IT WAS A DISCO PLACE FOR YOU AND ME
        ON THE DOOR YOU PAID YOUR MONEY
        THE PLACE WAS PACKED THE PLACE WAS
        FUNNY
        YOU SAW THE GIRLS
        MMMMM.... SMELLED THEIR HONEY
        THE HEADS WERE HAZY
        THE LIMBS WERE LAZY
        AND ALL THE YOUNG GIRLS DANCE LIKE
        CRAZY
        COME ON

BUT NOW IT'S OVER YOU GOTTA GO HOME
THERE IS NOWHERE ELSE TO ROAM
BE CAREFUL HOW YOU WALK THE STREETS
THEY'RE THE MEANEST STREETS IN THE
WHOLE DAMN PLACE
COME ON

WELL FRIDAY NIGHTS AND SATURDAYS
TOO
WE'LL BE DOWN HERE, YES, WITH YOU
AND YOU
AND YOU
AND YOU...

LES   Thank you and goodnight.

(Music comes up as the bouncers take their bow. They then usher out the audience much in the same way as they greeted the audience at the start, improvising suitable comments.)

SHAKERS

by John Godber and Jane Thornton

836

photograph by Tony Baines from the Hull Truck Theatre Company production of Shakers

SHAKERS was first presented by the Hull Truck Theatre Company at Spring Street Theatre, Hull, on 29 January 1984, with the following cast:

ADELE	Alison Grant
CAROL	Alison Watt
MEL	Marion Summerfield
NICKY	Sherry Baines

Directed by John Godber

AUTHORS' NOTE

In recent years cocktail and wine bars have sprung up all over the country. They attract a clientele which is as distinctive as that of the traditional public houses. Shakers is one of these trendy bars that can be seen in every major city in Britain. They provide an ironic means of escape from the gruelling pressures of life in the eighties; and from these tropical dreamworlds emerges a sad reality as observed by four female waitresses.

Shakers is more than a companion piece to *Bouncers*. In writing it we were attempting to create a popular piece of theatre which would communicate female issues to an audience who perhaps did not expect to encounter such concerns. Hence we opted for a humorous and observational approach. We also felt that we wanted to create a play that would offer exciting, physical and taxing roles for women. The amount of multi role-playing parts for actresses today are sadly few and far between.

As in *Bouncers* performances need to be sharp and heightened in order to make the passing scene changes well focused. Once again flexibility can be applied to the text so that the play is made to work for every different production. It is important that *Shakers* should be made to relate to your particular context. Keep it alive and make it work for you.

Jane Thornton
John Godber
1987

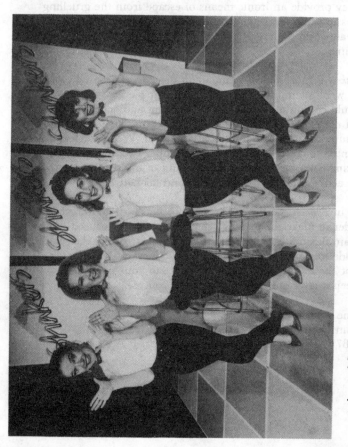

photograph by Tony Baines from the Hull Truck Theatre Company production of Shakers

SCENE ONE

Setting: Shakers cocktail bar. The setting is simple in order that attention is focused upon the actresses. A bar, positioned upstage, and four bar stools are all that are used to set the scene. The stools are moved around throughout the action whenever and wherever needed.

During the course of the action, the four waitresses, CAROL, MEL, NICKI and ADELE switch from role to role, playing the many characters who come into Shakers. Character changes and scene transitions should therefore be punctuated by music and lighting for full effect. In general, music and lighting play an integral part in the play and should be used imaginatively to convey the mood and atmosphere of the various scenes.

Whilst the audience enters, the actresses stand smoking, clearing away, stacking stools, etc. They address some of their remarks to the audience.

CAROL   I'm sorry. We're closed.

MEL   Yes. We *have* been here for seven hours.

NICKI   Don't remind me.

CAROL   You should have come earlier, love.

ADELE   Sorry.

NICKI   It's one o'clock in the bloody morning. What do they think we are?

MEL   It's because we're in the main street. You always get them, especially at weekends, trying to get a last drink as they're passing on the way to the taxi rank.

CAROL   Yes.

ADELE   It's because the lights are always on.

NICKI   Stupid that. Wastes electricity.

CAROL   Supposed to make it look classy.

NICKI   What a laugh.

MEL   Well, I'm off in a minute. I'm knackered.

ADELE   Day off tomorrow though.

CAROL   But it'll soon be Monday.

MEL   Oh, don't.

NICKI	I'm worn out, me. It's not right this. They need more waitresses. We shouldn't have to do everything.
CAROL	Yes. It's supposed to look all expensive and they can't even afford enough staff. It's all a façade.
NICKI	You're serving, making cocktails, fetching and carrying…
ADELE	And bloody smiling.

(The girls break out into the 'Shakers motif', (see photograph on page 61), as they introduce themselves. This involves holding an arm up to one side as if carrying a tray.)

CAROL	You've got Carol
ADELE	Adele
NICKI	Nicki
MEL	And Mel
CAROL	We work in a bar
ADELE	That is worse than hell
NICKI	We serve the drinks
MEL	And we serve the food
CAROL	We've got to be nice
ADELE	Not never ever rude
NICKI	No matter what you do
MEL	No matter what you say
CAROL	It's a happy smiling face
ADELE	That comes your way
ALL	'Ting'

(The girls from the 'Smiling motif', hands spread at each side of the mouth as if making it sparkle. See photo on page 65.)

SCENE TWO

MELANIE and ADELE are busy shaking, refilling and serving various cocktails. They speak in rhyme.

MEL	A taste of class
ADELE	In a Highball glass
MEL	Cocktails on ice
ADELE	That's nice
MEL	What're you making, Adele?
ADELE	What're you shaking, Mel?
MEL	Pass me a lemon slice
ADELE	You want a *Pina Colada?*
MEL	Oh, a *Vodka Hula!*
ADELE	*Tequila Sunrise!*
MEL	What? A *Southern Gin Cooler?*
ADELE	Got the ice in the shaker. Five cubes?
MEL	Or six?
ADELE	Fruit juice
MEL	Vermouth
ADELE	And vodka to mix
BOTH	Shake it all up 'til you form a frost It looks exciting Never mind the cost! 'Ting'

(NICKI *and* CAROL *become* DAZ *and* TREV.)

NICKI	Daz—
CAROL	Trev—
MEL	They've come down the bar
ADELE	To get themselves a bev
NICKI	And some skirt

(TREV *and* DAZ *are hanging around the cocktail bar. They are both about twenty-five, and working class. They are dressed up, and out for a good time.*)

NICKI	Go on then, Trev, ask her.
CAROL	You ask her.
NICKI	Ahhhhh! Chicken shit!
CAROL	I don't want a farty cocktail. I'd rather have a pint.
NICKI	It's a laugh though.
CAROL	Which one are you gonna ask?
NICKI	Her with the tits, not that other. She's too skinny.
CAROL	Yeh, that big one's alright.
ALL	Ugh.
NICKI	Nice jugs.

(*At this comment the girls feign being sick.*)

CAROL	You crude sod.
NICKI	Hey up, you can't deny it.
CAROL	How much are they?
NICKI	(*looking at* MEL's *breasts*) I don't think they're for sale.
CAROL	The drinks, dickhead.
NICKI	Two quid.
CAROL	It's not worth it.
NICKI	I'd like to see her face though.
CAROL	Loads of blokes will ask her for it. She won't bat an eyelid.
NICKI	Yes, but are they good-looking?
CAROL	Like you, you mean.
NICKI	You said it.
CAROL	Dream on...

(ADELE *and* MEL *are still mixing cocktails. They shout out the orders.*)

| MEL | One *Between the Sheets* and a *Bloody Mary*. What's that? |
| ADELE | *Zombie Voodoo*. |

MEL   Oooo they're awful them. They make my flesh creep.

ADELE   Why?

MEL   Well look at it. It's like sick, decorated with hundreds and thousands. I hate making them.

ADELE   They taste OK though. What are you making now?

MEL   *Harvey Wallbanger.*

ADELE   Nice.

MEL   I like making these.

ADELE   Easy aren't they? One *Zombie Voodoo*. Two quid love please. Thanks.

MEL   Do you want a lot of ice?

ADELE   So that's a *Screwdriver*. One *Johnny from London*.

NICKI   OK, guv.

ADELE   And one *Mary Stewart*.

CAROL   Och aye.

MEL   I'll just put a bit in then.

ADELE   Use the ashtray please love, or you'll ruin the carpet. (*To* MEL) Have you heard about the shorts?

MEL   Don't tell me we've to cut down on whisky again because it's getting too expensive.

ADELE   No, I mean shorts to wear.

MEL   You what?

ADELE   They want us to start wearing shorts from next month, like hot pant suits, you know.

MEL   With these shoes? You're joking.

ADELE   I'm not. Pass the Cherry Brandy.

MEL   It's bloody freezing in here as it is.

ADELE   I know. We'll be all goose pimply and white.

MEL   That's it then, I'm off on a diet.

ADELE   I'm off on a sunbed.

MEL	Do you have to wear them?
ADELE	I suppose so.
MEL	Shit.
ADELE	I'll go get some more ice.

(TREV and DAZ have approached MELANIE at the bar. She goes to serve them as ADELE exits.)

MEL	Are you being served?
CAROL	He wants one of them cocktails.
NICKI	Yes, one of them *cock*tails, love.
MEL	Which one do you fancy?
NICKI	*(looking at her breasts)* Well, they both look alright to me, pet.

(The two blokes laugh.)

CAROL	Excuse my friend, love. He doesn't know how to behave in front of ladies.
MEL	Yes, I noticed.
NICKI	I want a long comfortable screw…

(They laugh again.)

MEL	*(to the audience)* What a surprise! Regular or giant size?
NICKI	You what?
MEL	Big or small?
NICKI	Guess, love.
CAROL	Make a wish.

(They laugh again.)

MEL	*(to the audience)* The customer's always right. Just remember. Whatever.
CAROL	Sorry love. Just a joke.
MEL	Oh, is that what it was?
NICKI	Yeah funny, eh?
MEL	Funny.

CAROL   Don't smile much, do you?

MEL   I'm tired.

NICKI   Too much bed and no sleep, eh love?

MEL   Look, do you want a drink or not? I haven't got all night.

NICKI   How much are they?

MEL   Two quid for a small one, four for a big one.

NICKI   It's a right rip off.

CAROL   It's expensive isn't it, love?

MEL   You don't *have* to have one.

NICKI   Touchy.

MEL   I'm waiting.

CAROL   She's waiting.

NICKI   I'll have a small one.

MEL   With or without ice?

BOTH   With ice.

(MELANIE *speaks to the audience while preparing the cocktail.* CAROL *and* NICKI *mime the actions to the speech.*)

MEL   Bleedin' cocktails, it's the same every night. You always get an *Uptown Zombie,* with a *Glad Eye* and a *Pick Me Up,* promising a holiday with a *Tequila Sunrise* on *Montego Bay* and a ride on his *Pina Colada.* What he really means is that he'd like to give you a *Long Slow Comfortable Screw Between the Sheets* in his *Sidecar.* I'd just like to give the *Bosom Caresser* a *Sparkling Punch* in his *Dicki Dicki,* so he falls *Head Over Heels* and goes home clutching his *Blue Bols.* Two pound please, boys.

BOTH   Thanks.

MEL   You want a *Pina Colada.*

ADELE   Or a *Vodka Hula.*

MEL   *Tequila Sunrise.*

ADELE   A *Southern Gin Cooler.*

MEL	What ever you ask for
ADELE	We can make
MEL	Just give us a name
ADELE	And we'll give you a shake
BOTH	'Ting'
	(*Music*)

SCENE THREE

MEL *and* NICKI *become* SUSAN *and* ELAINE *working at supermarket checkout tills. Supermarket 'muzak' plays in the background.*

MEL	Susan—
NICKI	Elaine—
MEL	God, it's dragging.
NICKI	I know.
MEL	I hate it on the tills me. In the last half hour all I've had is an old woman with some bog rolls.
NICKI	It's always the same at this time of day.
MEL	Yeah, boring. I was supposed to be on the shop floor today doing cereals but they've put that bloody student on it, it makes me sick.
NICKI	It's not fair is it?
MEL	I mean she's only here for the holidays, I don't like her.
NICKI	No, I don't.
MEL	I wouldn't care, but I was loading bloody freezers all day yesterday, my hands nearly dropped off, it was that cold.
NICKI	They should give you gloves you know, you're not supposed to do it without gloves.
MEL	I know.

NICKI	But they don't care.
MEL	No.

(*Pause*)

NICKI	I'm looking forward to Mandy's party tomorrow night.
MEL	God, and me. I can't believe she's twenty-one, you know.
NICKI	Well you're not so far off.
MEL	Yes but it seems so old.
NICKI	Give over.
MEL	I'll tell you something. I might leave this job. I might do that hairdressing course at the tech that our Sandra's doing. She says it's great.
NICKI	You wouldn't have much money though, would you?
MEL	I've always fancied hairdressing though, it would be better than this.
NICKI	I suppose so.
MEL	Our Sandra's doing my hair for when we go out.
NICKI	Oh yes.
MEL	Crimping it.
NICKI	Oh.
MEL	What are you wearing?
NICKI	That black dress again I suppose?
MEL	It's nice that.
NICKI	It's alright.
MEL	Shaz and Tracey are getting all new stuff, aren't they?
NICKI	They must have more money than me then.
MEL	I might nip out to *Top Shop* in my dinner hour. It's posh is *Shakers*, you know, I need to get something smart.

NICKI	Yes.
MEL	Now that's something I wouldn't mind.
NICKI	What?
MEL	Working in a cocktail bar.

(*Music comes up as move back to Shakers for the next scene.*)

SCENE FOUR

NICKI	I think I've got a corn.
ADELE	What, on table four?
CAROL	Sweetcorn?
NICKI	No. On my foot.
MEL	Give over.
NICKI	It's killing me.
CAROL	Stop wingeing.
NICKI	Right on my little toe.
MEL	I've just served two right prats.
ADELE	So what's new.
MEL	Guess what they asked for?
ALL	A long slow comfortable screw?
MEL	You said it.
CAROL	Typical.
MEL	And they were on about my tits, bastards.
NICKI	Strong words.
MEL	Listen at the kettle calling the frying pan black.
ADELE	You see that bloke over there with the nose and the glasses?
ALL	Yes.

ADELE   He's been dying to ask me for a *Screw*, but every time
        he comes to the bar he chickens out and asks for some
        peanuts.

CAROL   Good job by the looks of him.

ADELE   I wouldn't care but he's had ten packets!

NICKI   Well, with them peanuts and that chilli he'll pebble-
        dash the toilets.

ALL   Ugh Nicki?

NICKI   What's up?

SCENE FIVE

MEL   One *Bossa Nova*

ADELE   One *Pina Colada*

NICKI   One 'Happy Hour' from six till seven
        One brace of TV producers
        One would-be actress, thank you

        (MEL, ADELE *and* CAROL *become TV producers,* WILLY,
        MERVYN *and* GERRY.)

MEL   Urm...urm...OK — what do you have?

NICKI   What would you like, sir?

MEL   Too early for any of that, thanks...

        (*The producers all laugh.*)

NICKI   Sorry?

MEL   Never mind. I'll have a...a... (*goes into a freeze whilst
        trying to decide on a drink.*)

NICKI   You wait for hours until the silly oaf has decided what
        he wants. First he'll choose a lager.

MEL   I'll have a lager.

NICKI   Then change his mind because of his blood pressure.

MEL   No, no, no...must think about the old blood pressure.

NICKI   And you nod...like you're concerned. (*She nods, concerned.*)

MEL   I think I'll have a...

NICKI   He'll go for the Martini.

MEL   Martini.

NICKI   I knew it.

MEL   Really.

NICKI   (*to audience*) With lemonade and ice.

MEL   With...

NICKI   Lemonade and ice, sir?

MEL   How marvellous...

NICKI   So it's served and he says to his mates that he's got a double measure.

MEL   I've got a double measure.

NICKI   That's 'Happy Hour', sir. Six till seven, double measure for the price of one.

MEL   What's everyone else having? Urm Gerry? Mervyn?

CAROL   Gerry—

ADELE   Mervyn—

MEL   What are you having? What's your poison?

NICKI   They've just been looking at a new car outside.

ADELE   We've just been looking at a new car outside.

MEL   What're you having?

ADELE   Martini...

CAROL   And me, Willy.

MEL   Three Martinis, lovey.

NICKI   I wince and smile, lovey. Shit?

          (NICKI *serves the drinks. The others drink them in graphic fashion.*)

CAROL   Wonderful.

ADELE   Didn't touch the sides. Lovely motor out there.

MEL   Same again? Gerry? Mervyn?

ADELE   Oh I don't know.

CAROL   I have a long drive.

ADELE   Oh, what the hell.

CAROL   Same again.

(*They raise their fingers to order.*)

NICKI   And before they can utter the order...wooosh — three Martinis.

MEL   With lemonade?

NICKI   Yes sir.

(*The three drink up, stumble backwards, laugh and come together. They now seem lubricated enough to start their chat.*)

CAROL   God, what a day.

MEL   Really?

ADELE   Hasn't it just.

CAROL   We're working in studio one.

ADELE   It's such a bloody effort.

MEL   Who's directing?

CAROL   Brian.

ALL   Oh God!

CAROL   What a prick. Honestly it takes the man forever to do a two minute scene.

ADELE   He likes to feel that he's being taken seriously. He's straight out of Oxford and straight into the Beeb.

NICKI   Aren't they all?

CAROL   The script's a dream.

NICKI   They're talking louder now. The name-dropping follows shortly.

MEL   Aren't you two working on the new Bleasdale project?

CAROL	Yes, that's right. I'm producing. Mervyn's assistant.
MEL	And Brian's directing that?
CAROL	I think that's what he calls it.
ADELE	It's an excellent cast.
MEL	Isn't urm…
CAROL	Another, Willy?
MEL	Please.
CAROL	Three more please, lovey.
ADELE	No ice in mine, it goes through me.
MEL	Julie Walters?
ADELE	Yes, she's marvellous.
CAROL	Oh she's wonderful in it, Julie Walters.
NICKI	Excuse me, did you say Julie Walters?
CAROL	Yes, she's marvellous in it.
MEL	The camera likes her.
ADELE	Oh absolutely.
CAROL	Which is more than can be said for the other one.
	(*Laughter.*)
MEL	How's the Volvo?
ADELE	Changed it.
MEL	Really?
ADELE	Got myself a new Sierra 4XR.
MEL	How do you find it?
ADELE	Well I just open the garage and there it is.
	(*Laughter.*)
MEL	Oh brilliant. Another, everyone? Same again, lovey.
	(*The drinks arrive.*)
MEL	Pretty girl; wouldn't mind a bash at it.
CAROL	Yes, whorish but innocent.

ADELE   Sort of drawn but nubile.

          (*Laughter.*)

MEL   Aren't they awkward on the road?

CAROL   More awkward in bed?

MEL   I meant the car. More's the pity.

ADELE   No, no, they're fine.

MEL   I'm still with the old Rover.

CAROL   How's Vicky, Willy?

MEL   Oh, shit!

CAROL   What's the matter?

MEL   Vicky. Hell, must ring the old girl. Shan't be a mo.

          (MEL *makes for an imaginary phone in order to phone*
          VICKY. *The* OTHERS *become* VICKY's *voice interjecting into*
          the conversation. The voice should sound like a fast-forward
          taped voice, garbled and speedy with the occasional recognisable
          word as indicated.)

MEL   Hello, Vicky darling…

OTHERS   Blah…blah…blah…bastard.

MEL   It's Will. Listen lovey, sorry to be such an awful
          drag…

OTHERS   Blah…blah…blah…drag.

MEL   …but something's cropped up.

          (*The* OTHERS *laugh as* GERRY *and* MERVYN.)

MEL   No, lovey, still at the studio.

OTHERS   Blah…blah…blah…studio.

MEL   We're having a bit of a scene with one of the
          scriptwriters. He's having a bit of a fit.

OTHERS   Blah…blah…blah…ooh err.

MEL   It might take forever.

          (*The* OTHERS *laugh.*)

MEL   No, of course I'm not in a bar, darling.

(*Music comes up as* NICKI, CAROL, ADELE *and* MEL *all become waitresses once more.*)

NICKI   I'm not kidding, it's stupid in this place.

CAROL   We know.

NICKI   First you're on cocktails, then you're serving. You don't know whether you're coming or going.

ADELE   Yeah, I don't know my John Collins from my bolognese.

MEL   I don't know my head from my arse.

NICKI   Hey, have you heard about the shorts?

CAROL   Yes.

NICKI   Yes.

MEL   Well, I'm not wearing shorts with these shoes. He's bloody had it.

CAROL   You know what'll be next, don't you?

ALL   No what?

CAROL   Topless.

ALL   Never.

CAROL   We'll start with shorts, then camiknickers, then it'll be tutus like those big London places, then topless…

NICKI   Urrrrgggg God!

CAROL   It's TRUE. Monday to Wednesday. To help boost custom, I bet you.

ADELE   Well I don't think I'd boost custom very much.

NICKI   Isn't it pathetic?

CAROL   You wait and see.

NICKI   Well I'll not be here then.

MEL   You hope.

NICKI   Would you do it then, Mel?

MEL   Would I hell. I'm not common. In fact, the mood I'm in, if somebody looks at my tits again I'll poke their eyes out!

CAROL   Good for you.

ADELE   Hey look at them. Silly so and sos.

NICKI   Where?

ADELE   Table seven.

MEL   Oh yeah, fancy dress. Bet they're off to a disco.

NICKI   What are they supposed to be?

ADELE   God knows.

NICKI   Oh, look, a frog.

(They all mimic the croak of a frog. Pause. They then once more become TV producers.)

MEL   No Vicky, just a couple of actors, blasted things, going over their lines. A new series about a cocktail bar.

OTHERS   Blah...blah...blah...Cocktail bar.

MEL   Love you, darling. Must dash. Oh, it's absolute chaos down here. You'd have a fit. You wouldn't believe it. No, of course not. I'll eat out. Love you.

OTHERS   Blah...blah...blah...Love you.

ADELE   How is Vicky?

MEL   She is just the most marvellous woman I know.

CAROL   Wish I could say the same for mine. The old bat.

ADELE   Oh look at the pissing time. Another drink chaps, whilst it's reasonable?

MEL   I'd say. Same again, my lovey.

NICKI   By this time, you've plucked up enough courage to actually speak to them. Excuse me, you from the telly?

CAROL   Yes we are?

ADELE   How did you guess?

NICKI   *(to audience)* And then you're forced to say something stupid and crass like — I dunno.

(They laugh.)

| NICKI | And they laugh, like you've just told the funniest joke since the one about a man with a sheep's head. |

ADELE   And he says to the butcher, "do you have a sheep's head?," and the butcher says, "no, it's just the way I comb my hair."

(*Laughter*.)

NICKI   Yeah, just like that.

MEL   Are you interested in acting?

NICKI   Oh yeah. I'd like to be an actress.

MEL   What about this job, it must be interesting, meeting jetsetting people like ourselves.

NICKI   I want to say, "No I hate this job; the hours are awful, the customers less than polite. They treat you like shit, but unemployment is so high that any job is a job"...but I really say... "Oh it's alright really, I suppose."

MEL   You take some of my advice, don't put your daughter on the stage...

ALL   Mrs Worthington.

MEL   Now then, I bet you can't tell me who said that, can you?

NICKI   Noel Coward?

MEL   Oh.

NICKI   It was only a guess. But it made me feel better.

CAROL   Last one. One for the road.

(*They down another drink for the road.*)

ADELE   I must say, I feel good.

CAROL   And me.

MEL   I feel fine.

NICKI   I feel like the evening is just starting. And it is, better sneak a wine.

ALL   Have a good audition, lovey.

(*Music*)

SCENE SIX

ADELE   I've seen a ring in the *Argos* catalogue.

NICKI   How much is it?

ADELE   Well I don't want a big one. They don't suit me.

MEL   Come on, how much?

ADELE   About eighty quid, but it don't look cheap.

NICKI   When are you getting it?

ADELE   Saturday.

CAROL   I think you're stupid.

ADELE   What for?

CAROL   Wasting your life.

MEL   It's her life, Carol.

NICKI   And he does love her, I mean it's serious.

CAROL   Oh yeah?

ADELE   Why is it a waste?

CAROL   It doesn't matter.

MEL   Go on.

NICKI   Say what you were going to say.

CAROL   It's just that there's more to life than getting married. There's places to go, things to see. You could make something for yourself.

ADELE   Like you, you mean?

CAROL   You've got to keep trying.

MEL   Why, what have you got, Carol?

CAROL   Okay, I'm sorry I'm wrong.

NICKI   You should be. You're supposed to be clever, been to college and that. If you're that clever, what're doing working here?

CAROL   I don't know.

MEL   At least she's got a boyfriend.

         (*Spotlight on* CAROL.)

CAROL   When I was sixteen, all my close friends left school to
         work in factories. I stayed on; I thought it would lead
         to something better. Well everybody said it would; my
         mum, dad, teachers. To them exams were everything.
         It was hard making new friends in the Sixth form.
         They seemed different to me. Their mams and dads
         were doctors, teachers, they all seemed to be better.
         My mam delivered milk. Oh, I got all my 'A' levels.
         I've got a degree in Modern Studies from Lancaster
         Poly. I had a good time at the Poly; I fell in love, out
         of love, was left devastated for a term, smoked dope,
         wore cheap plimsolls, and bought a cheap fur coat, uh
         uh. I made some good friends. Funny how they all
         disappear when you leave. It's like you've never
         known them. You've lived in a world with everything,
         then you're dumped into the wilderness. Nobody's
         ever heard of Modern Studies out here, and to me it
         was everything. Competing for jobs with computer
         and mathematical geniuses, I don't stand a chance.
         Or you're overqualified. I nearly didn't get this job. I
         did nannying for a bit, but the pay was rubbish, so I
         came home, and I'm here. I saw a girl who was in
         my class at school yesterday. She's got two kids.

NICKI   Aren't they nice?

MEL   How old is he?

ADELE   Eighteen months.

CAROL   One's walking. She was laughing and playing with
         them. They'd got chocolate round their mouths. I
         looked at her and I thought, well, she seems to have
         got what she wanted, and I suppose I've got what I
         wanted, a degree in Modern Studies.

         (*Music*)

SCENE SEVEN

*Typical shop disco music plays in the background to convey
where we now are.* ADELE *and* CAROL *become* SHARON *and*
TRACEY *buying their outfits for the night out.* MEL *becomes a
girl trying on clothes.* NICKI *becomes the shop assistant.*

ALL	Chelsea Girl
ADELE	Sharon—
CAROL	Tracey—
MEL	Girl in shop—
NICKI	Assistant—
ADELE	It's for Mandy's party at *Shakers*.
CAROL	Do you have to get dressed up?
ADELE	I am.
CAROL	I might not go yet.
ADELE	I'm going because Andy King's going to be there.
CAROL	Is he?
ADELE	I think so.
CAROL	I'm off then.
ADELE	Keep your hands off him you cheeky gett.
NICKI	How many have you got there, love?
CAROL	Two pairs of jeans.
NICKI	Take this shirt in with you, love.
CAROL	Yes.
NICKI	It's three garments.
CAROL	Thanks.
NICKI	Just through there. Three love?
ADELE	Yes.
NICKI	In you go.
ADELE ⎫ CAROL ⎭	Get her.

(NICKI *becomes another girl trying on clothes.*)

CAROL   I hate these communal ones. Everybody looks at you. (*looking round*) I don't like what she's got on.

ADELE   I've got one of them.

CAROL   Well it's not so bad. Just doesn't suit her probably.

ADELE   No.

CAROL   Have you heard this music? Chuffin' hell.

ADELE   Duran Duran; it's great.

CAROL   Not in here though. Feels like Simon le Bon's watching you get changed.

ADELE   You should be so lucky.

CAROL   Mind you he'd probably be sick if he saw me get changed with my legs.

ADELE   There's nowt wrong with your legs.

CAROL   There is. They're massive.

ADELE   You're just paranoid.

CAROL   They are though, look.

ADELE   You're daft.

CAROL   Mind you, when you look at her over there, I don't suppose mine are that bad.

ADELE   Where?

CAROL   In that corner.

ADELE   Oh I wouldn't dare.

CAROL   She's no idea.

ADELE   Trying a mini skirt on with a figure like that.

CAROL   She looks a right state.

ADELE   It's like trying to pack your suitcase when you're off on holiday.

CAROL   What?

ADELE   Her trying to get into that.

(*They both laugh. Throughout the whole of this sequence they both gradually mime undressing and trying on.*)

CAROL   Look at that one. She's got no bra on.

ADELE   Dirty bitch. Who does she think she is?

CAROL   Makes my nipples sore, that.

ADELE   What?

CAROL   Not wearing a bra.

ADELE   I wish I'd put some decent knickers on.

CAROL   I wish I'd shaved my legs.

ADELE   She's nice.

CAROL   Who?

ADELE   You can see her in the mirror. Nice figure.

ALL   Oh yeah.

CAROL   Wish I looked like that. The cow.

ADELE   She's got a bit of a dog face though.

CAROL   Ugly.

ADELE   Yeah.

GIRL   Excuse me. What does this look like?

ADELE   Looks nice.

CAROL   It's alright.

GIRL   I'm by myself you see, and I can't decide.

ADELE   It's nice.

GIRL   I've been looking in this mirror for ages. I'm not sure
        about this low-cut back.

ADELE   Suits you.

GIRL   Do you think so?

ADELE   It'll look great for a disco.

GIRL   That's what I thought.

ADELE   You can't go wrong.

GIRL   I think I'll have it then. Thanks a lot.

ADELE   That's alright.

CAROL   It looked naff, that dress.

ADELE	I know.
CAROL	Vile colour.
ADELE	Awful!
CAROL	Why didn't you tell her?
ADELE	Why didn't you?
CAROL	She didn't ask me.
ADELE	You can't though, can you?
CAROL	Did you see all them spots on her back?
ADELE	Horrible weren't they?
CAROL	She should get a dress to cover them up, not one like that.
ADELE	Yes she should, some people have no taste.
CAROL	Poor cow. What a waste of money.
ADELE	What's this dress look like?
CAROL	Oooh, it looks lovely that.
ADELE	Does it, or are you having me on?
CAROL	No it does.
ADELE	Really?
CAROL	Yes, it's flattering.
ADELE	I quite like it.
CAROL	It will look better with stilettos instead of them trainers.
ADELE	I know that, stupid. I don't know whether I like that one she's trying on better.
CAROL	Oh no, it looks cheap that. Get that, it suits you.

(*For the last page or so* TRACEY *has desperately been trying to get some jeans on.*)

CAROL	I can't get these jeans on me.
ADELE	What size are they?
CAROL	A ten.
ADELE	They should fit.

CAROL   It's my legs. I've told you.

ADELE   They're probably small fitting.

CAROL   It's no good. I can't suck my legs in.

ADELE   Lie on the floor.

CAROL   They're meant for people with no legs.

ADELE   You what?

CAROL   This style, it's meant for people like you with no legs.

ADELE   Skinny legs you mean?

CAROL   You know what I mean.

ADELE   Lie down. They'll zip up then. That's what I do with mine.

CAROL   I'll feel stupid.

ADELE   Lie down.

(CAROL *painfully lies down on the floor. The two girls begin to giggle.*)

ADELE   I'll hold them together at the waist and you try and pull up the zip.

CAROL   Alright.

ADELE   Breathe in.

CAROL   I am, you cheeky cow.

ADELE   It's no good. It won't go.

CAROL   I told you.

(NICKI *stares.*)

CAROL   What's she looking at?

ADELE   Take no notice.

CAROL   Just because she's thin.

ADELE   Don't start, Tracey.

CAROL   Well. At least I'm shapely. She's like a bit of string.

ADELE   Shut up and try a bigger size.

CAROL   Are you having that dress, Shaz?

ADELE   I think so.

CAROL   You ought to. It's nice.

ADELE   I think I will. I'll get some of them diamante earrings
        to go with it.

CAROL   Will you wait while I try some more jeans on first?

ADELE   Well hurry up.

CAROL   (*leaning out to the assistant with her coat hanger.*) Excuse
        me could you swop me these for a size twelve?

NICKI   I'm sorry. We've no twelves left in that style.

CAROL   Have you got any large fitting tens?

NICKI   All our tens are small fitting.

CAROL   What about a small fitting fourteen.

NICKI   All out of fourteens. They've been ever so popular.
        There should be some more in next week sometime.

CAROL   I might call back then.

NICKI   Sorry.

CAROL   I liked them as well. Let's go to the C & A.

        (*Music*)

SCENE EIGHT

MEL   My mum tells everyone that I work in *Shakers*. She
        thinks it's classy. Well it is. I keep saying, I'll bring
        her, treat her. She says she'll have to go out and buy
        a new frock. It's not that posh I tell her. It would do
        her good to come out somewhere like this, glam'
        herself up a bit. She's not been the same since my
        dad died, about a year ago now. She misses him, still
        talks to him sometimes, when she's in bed you know.
        Funny that, but I suppose you get used to people
        being there. She goes to the Bingo on Wednesdays
        with my Auntie Eileen, and she babysits for our
        Kevin's kids. Yes she'd like it here, somewhere
        special. Maybe I'll bring her next week. I'm getting
        used to it now, when I first started, well...

ADELE   Mel's first day in the kitchen.

ALL   "Ting"

MEL   "Ting"

MEL   I'd always wanted to work in *Shakers*, ever since it first opened two years ago. At that time I was working in the *Red Lion*.

ALL   (*sing*) "Stand by your man"

MEL   Different clientele.

         (MEL *mimes pulling a pint.* NICKI *and* CAROL *play darts.* ADELE *becomes a clock.*)

NICKI   180.

CAROL   2.

MEL   Sixty-nine, please, Ken.

ADELE   It's a bit quiet tonight, Melanie sunshine.

         (*They all cough loudly.*)

MEL   Yes.

ADELE   Mind you, we could liven it up if we wanted, couldn't we?

         (*They all cough loudly.*)

MEL   We could, yes. Old Ken was in the *Red Lion* from seven till eleven every night.

ADELE   I like a steady pint.

MEL   There was no life in the *Red Lion*. Business was bad in the pubs. They were dead, and so were some of the conversations.

ADELE   I've seen a lovely piece of wood today.

MEL   Oh yes.

ADELE   I was telling Ron, weren't I Ron, up on that there tip, there's some smashing wood. I was thinking of going and getting myself a piece, and shaving it down and making our lass a cabinet. Yes there's some great wood up on that tip, and it's all rubbish, thrown away. Money to burn, they must have. I say money to burn.

CAROL   Ooh.

MEL   Sometimes it would get very heated in the *Red Lion* especially when the fishing trip started arguing.

ALL   What? No! Never! Cheers Melanie.

CAROL   Four barrels for twelve quid.

NICKI   Rubbish.

CAROL   I'm telling yer.

NICKI   Go and have an operation. You need one.

CAROL   I'm telling you. I can get four barrels for twelve quid.

NICKI   You can't get me four barrels.

CAROL   I'm telling you. Four barrels of creosote, twelve quid.

NICKI   Creosote for that price. I don't believe it.

CAROL   I'm telling you.

NICKI   Right, get me two barrels.

MEL   So *Shakers* was a shock.

ALL   "Ting"

MEL   "Ting"

(*Return to Shakers. The actresses mime a sequence to music, to convey the bustling atmosphere and* MEL's *confusion at life as a waitress. The actresses become swing doors, etc.* MEL *drops things, trips, etc. She eventually uncorks some champagne and is saved by the others rushing to her aid and recorking it. The noise eventually stops.*)

MEL   Everyone was really helpful.

ALL   Smile!

(*For the next three lines,* ADELE, NICKI *and* CAROL *become mad chefs, gesticulating and shouting wildly behind an imaginary bar.*)

NICKI   Two specials, one lasagne

CAROL   Three chips, two sirloin, one rump

ADELE   One spag bol, one 'T' bone special

MEL	It was like working in a nightmare. (*She shouts.*) One Chip Cocktail, one Prawn Bread, one Garlic Orange, a Side Mushroom, one Steak Pasta and a bowl of Special K.

(*As MEL's speech finishes, the others break out of their roles. The atmosphere slows down.*)

CAROL	It's. OK. You'll get the hang of it.
MEL	I feel so stupid.
ADELE	Don't worry, you'll get over it. I was the same when I first started.
MEL	You weren't?
ADELE	Yes, I once ordered garlic mushrooms, lasagne and spag bol.
CAROL	Yeah?
MEL	Well, what was wrong with that?
ADELE	I was working in a Chinese restaurant at the time.
NICKI	Yeah I know what you mean. Half of the time I shout out the first thing I see.
CAROL	You would.
MEL	I don't know how they eat it so quickly. I'd get indigestion.
CAROL	It's all kelp induced food anyway.
NICKI	You what?
CAROL	Kelp.
NICKI	Sounds like a Beatles' track.
NICKI	Kelp, I need somebody.
CAROL	When's your audition?
NICKI	I haven't heard yet.
MEL	Hadn't we better get back?
ADELE	Oh shit!
CAROL	What's up?
ADELE	I was supposed to get a table ready for a birthday party coming in at nine.

SCENE NINE

ALL   Getting ready for the party

ADELE   Sharon—

CAROL   Tracey—

MEL   Susan—

NICKI   Elaine—

(*Music comes up as the girls all freeze into a position relating to getting ready for a night out.* NICKI *is ironing;* CAROL *is under a sun lamp;* ADELE *has a face mask.* MEL *enters.*)

MEL   Hey up, I'm here. Chuffin' buses; they're never on time. They make me sick. I've brought my heated rollers and my hot brush. I've got some mousse but I couldn't find my gel, so you'll have to lend me some. I've got some of them *More* cigarettes as well; long and brown, I think they look great. Let's have a look at your dress then Shaz. Got it from *Chelsea Girl* didn't you? Where's Tracey and Elaine? Are you talking, or what?

ADELE   (*through an almost closed mouth, as she is wearing a face mask*) I can't.

MEL   You what?

ADELE   I can't.

MEL   Uggh. What's that stuff on your face?

ADELE   Face mask. (*She points to an imaginary bottle.*)

MEL   (*Picking bottle up and reading*) "Avocado and Cucumber — the first step to a more beautiful you." I'll tell you something, it's definitely working. You look a stack better with that on than you ever did before.

ADELE   Don't make me laugh.

MEL   Ahhh, don't move, it's cracking.

ADELE   Don't make me laugh.

MEL   Too late, it's gone.

ADELE	Shit!
MEL	You'll be right.
ADELE	Well, I have had it on ages. (*She mimes removing the face mask, making the appropriate noises.*)
NICKI	(*coming out of her freeze*) I've finished with the ironing board, Shaz, so I've folded it up and put it in that cupboard. Hiya Susan!
MEL	Hi. (*To audience.*) She gets right up my arse.
NICKI	(*to audience*) She gets right on my tits. (*To* MEL.) Late, aren't you?
MEL	Buses.
NICKI	I came in my dad's car.
MEL	You would.
CAROL	(*coming out of her freeze*) What am I gonna do? Look at my face!
NICKI	It's bright red!
CAROL	I know that.
MEL	What's happened?
ADELE	She's been on the sun lamp.
ALL	Ohh er...
CAROL	I only stayed five minutes.
ADELE	You're not used to it.
MEL	It's because you've got fair skin.
CAROL	I can't go out like this.
NICKI	Powder it down.
CAROL	I can try.
ADELE	I'm going to have a bath. (*She uses the bar as the bath.*)
MEL	Shit. There's a ladder in my tights.
CAROL	I've got to shave my armpits yet.
MEL	And I only bought them today.
NICKI	I've got some spare ones in my bag.

MEL	They won't fit me.
ADELE	They fit any size.
MEL	Do they?
NICKI	Yes.
CAROL	Have you got any Immac?
ADELE	In the bathroom.
CAROL	Thanks.
NICKI	I'll have to cover up my spots.
CAROL	I'll have to cover up my face.
MEL	Can I borrow some perfume? I forgot mine.
ADELE	Plug your heated rollers in. I'll need them when I come out of the bath.
MEL	They're new — Braun.
NICKI	They won't work if your hair's wet.
ALL	Seen 'em on the telly.
ADELE	I know. I'll dry it first.
CAROL	Will you put my nail varnish on for me? I can't do it with my left hand.
NICKI	Can I borrow your mascara?
MEL	Do I look fat in this dress?
ADELE	You look alright.
CAROL	I look like a tomato.
ADELE	Do you think Andy King will turn up?
ALL	God Andy King!
NICKI	Why?
ADELE	Just wondered.
MEL	Oh yes.
CAROL	Can you see my blackheads?
MEL	You think you've got problems.

CAROL	Have you got anything for bad breath?
ALL	Oh we'll never be ready.

(Music)

POSSIBLE INTERVAL

SCENE TEN

NICKI *is wearing shorts.*

ADELE	What have you got them on for?
NICKI	From Monday, he said.
CAROL	So?
NICKI	So that's why I've got them on.
CAROL	I thought that we agreed that we weren't going to wear them.
ADELE	Yes, we did.
MEL	I'm not...I am not.
NICKI	I think they're alright.
CAROL	You would.
NICKI	And what's that supposed to mean?
CAROL	Forget it.
MEL	Can't we just ask him about them first? I mean it's alright for you, Nicki, but I'd feel embarrassed.
ADELE	I don't like them. They're a funny shape.
NICKI	I don't know what you're fussing about.
CAROL	It's degrading. It's only so men can look at your arse, you know.
ADELE	I think she's right Nicki. It's just to try to get more customers.
NICKI	Is it chuff?
CAROL	Well, why do you think we have to wear them?

NICKI	'Cos it's getting warmer; to make us look more summery that's all.
CAROL	You're bloody thick.
NICKI	At least I'm not ashamed of my body.
CAROL	Why don't you get your tits out then while you're at it? You might as well.
NICKI	Piss off!
MEL	Oh don't start, just forget it. If she wants to wear them, let her wear them. It's her that looks stupid.
CAROL	Look, if she wears them we'll all have to.
MEL	Why?
CAROL	Because she's setting a precedent.
ADELE	A what?
CAROL	He'll say that if they're good enough for Nicki, they're good enough for all of us.
NICKI	Hang on, hang on, don't start blaming me. I'm just doing my job. He's told us to wear them, so I am.
CAROL	I suppose you'd shave your head as well if he told you.
NICKI	I might do.
CAROL	He can't make us wear them you know.
MEL	But what if he sacks us?
CAROL	What all of us? Come on...
ADELE	Hey, he might.
CAROL	Go take them off, Nicki.
NICKI	Just mind your own business, will you.
ADELE	But they do look daft, especially with them shoes.
MEL	Yes, they do.
CAROL	Take them off. Think about somebody else but yourself for a change.
NICKI	What do you mean?

CAROL   Well, why should us three wear them when we don't
         want to, just because you fancy yourself in them?
         You're outnumbered. Take them off.

NICKI   Threatening me now, are you? Well I'm not scared of
         you.

CAROL   You're a silly cow!

NICKI   Look, if you can't cope with the job why don't you
         leave? Mind you, this is the only job you could get as
         it is, isn't it?

CAROL   Fuck off!

NICKI   And you!

ADELE   Nicki, be reasonable will you.

CAROL   If you don't take them off, I'll rip them off you.

NICKI   Don't make me laugh.

CAROL   I mean it.

         (*Pause.*)

NICKI   Alright, alright, I'll take them off. I'll take the bloody
         things off if it will please you, if it will stop you going
         on. (*She goes to take them off behind the bar.*) It was only a
         joke anyway. But you don't know what a joke is, do
         you, Carol? If you laughed you'd shit yourself. (*She
         comes back out with her trousers on.*) Better?

SCENE ELEVEN

CAROL   And in they come, straight out of the car, straight
         into the bar

ADELE   The boys, is what they are, dressed in their best,
         Stonewash jeans

MEL   All talced and fresh, with splash-on Aramis, minty
         foot deodorant, and teeth gleaming white like George
         Michael

ALL   "Wake me up before you go go"

NICKI   It's cold outside but they don't care
           A Bermuda 'T' shirt is all they wear

CAROL   Let's get to the bar. Hi.

ADELE   Hi teamsters.

MEL   Hi.

NICKI   Hi.

CAROL   They stand like they're in a shop window. Got to get the most out of their jeans. Yeah that's it. That looks cool and attractive without being cissy or macho.

(They all take up different stances.)

ADELE   A sort of cross between Simon le Bon and Daley Thompson.

MEL   And the gum, don't forget the gum.

ALL   Oh yes, the gum.

(They all pretend to chew gum.)

NICKI   In goes the gum.

ALL   Thud; Chew.

ADELE   And the casual look around the place, eyeing up everything that moves.

MEL   If it moves, take it to bed; if not, stick it on your windscreen.

NICKI   Trev and Val, *Radio One Road Show*.

CAROL   Sound your horn if you had sex last night.

ALL   *(making horn sounds)* Road hog.

ADELE   And then I spot one. Oh yes, over there by the cig machine; big tits, no tights. Slit up her dress, hair like one of those dancers from *Top of the Pops*.

CAROL   Where is she?

ADELE   Over my left shoulder, two o'clock to the bar, five o'clock to the cig machine.

CAROL   Nice one.

ADELE   So over to the ciggy machine I glide.

(ADELE *glides over to* MEL *at the cigarette machine.*)

MEL   Shit!

ADELE   Isn't it working?

MEL   No.

ADELE   Let me have a quick look. A masculine boot should get this going. Boot. There we are—twenty John Player Specials.

MEL   I wanted Benson and Hedges. Thanks anyway.

ADELE   She walks off. Shit! Lost my cool. Back to the teamsters.

NICKI   What happened, man?

ADELE   Oh what a dog!

MEL   She looks great.

ADELE   Up close she's really rough.

CAROL   And then like confetti, excuses hit the ground, falling on deaf ears.

ADELE   She's married.

MEL   She's fat.

CAROL   She's deaf.

ADELE   She's blind. She broke my cool. No problem—I'll laugh it off with a round of *Malibus*. A round of *Malibus*.

ALL   Hoorah!

CAROL   What happened? What went wrong? The ciggy machine chat-up always works. It was beautifully timed and wonderfully executed. Post-mortem is required. Did you shave?

ADELE   With Philips.

MEL   What about teeth?

ADELE   Spearmint mouthwash.

NICKI   Armpits?

ADELE   Yardley roll-on.

CAROL	Hair?
ADELE	Styled at Steiners.
MEL	Maybe...
ALL	What?
MEL	Maybe she wasn't interested?
ALL	Don't talk crap.
ADELE	Lets have another *Malibu*.
ALL	Yeah.
	(*Music*)

SCENE TWELVE

ADELE	Why don't you just come out and tell him?
MEL	I can't. I know he's awful to me, but there's something about him.
CAROL	But if he's been like that.
NICKI	Like what?
CAROL	Can I tell her?
MEL	I suppose so.
CAROL	Well if you don't want me to.
NICKI	Oh don't bother. I wasn't interested anyway.
ADELE	Nicki...
MEL	If you must know, I thought I was pregnant.
NICKI	Oh God.
ADELE	And he said that he was leaving her, that it was her fault.
NICKI	'Cos you were pregnant?
MEL	Yes.
NICKI	And are you?
MEL	No, but that's not the point.

ADELE	It's not right though is it.
MEL	I mean he's supposed to care about me.
CAROL	Don't put up with it, Mel.
MEL	It's difficult.
CAROL	He's using you.
NICKI	I'd just tell him to piss off.
MEL	Who the hell asked you, Bonny Langford?
NICKI	Christ, I only said...
MEL	I know what you said. Just keep your beak out.
NICKI	I like how I get all the aggro.
ADELE	Steady Mel, we're only saying...
MEL	Okay, okay sorry. Sorry Nicki.
NICKI	Yeah. I should think so.
MEL	I'm sorry.
NICKI	It's always Nicki.
MEL	I said I'm sorry.
NICKI	It's never Adele or Carol. It's always little Nicki.
MEL	I said I'm bloody sorry, alright.
NICKI	Oh let's have a go at Nicki. Let's use Nicki as the scapegoat. Just because you're having some male problems I'm the scapegoat.
MEL	Nicki?
NICKI	What?
MEL	I'm sorry.
ADELE	I think she knows now.
NICKI	Yeah well...
CAROL	He *is* using you Mel.
MEL	I know. I admit I am being used. Fine, great, excellent.

ADELE	All you have to do is say, "Peter, I know that you're married and that you're seeing the manageress of the supermarket, but you'll have to make a decision. It's either me or those two." It's that easy.
NICKI	And don't forget to get your key to the flat.
CAROL	And your stereo.
ADELE	And cassette.
NICKI	And radio alarm.
CAROL	And your car keys.
ADELE	Oh, and your portable telly.
	(*Pause.*)
MEL	You're right; he's using me.
NICKI	At least you're not pregnant. That's one thing.
MEL	Yes, I suppose so.
NICKI	That would have been the pits.
MEL	Yes. (*She forces a smile.*)
CAROL	It's awful when you think you are though, isn't it?
MEL	You can say that again.
CAROL	I once thought I was.
NICKI	And me.
ADELE	Yes...
CAROL	You see I took an orange pill on a Tuesday instead of a white one on a Thursday.
NICKI	I forgot to take some altogether.
ALL	Whoooo...
MEL	It's so easy when you're tired.
CAROL	I began to panic.
ALL	We know the feeling.
CAROL	I kept seeing...
ADELE	Round pregnant women?
MEL	Mothers with pushchairs.

CAROL   Isn't he nice?

NICKI   And adverts for abortion.

CAROL   Friendly—

MEL   Confidential—

NICKI   And free pregnancy tests—

ALL   Shit!

NICKI   Counted the weeks in my diary.

ADELE   Which days did I have sex?

MEL   I thought I was probably highly fertile.

CAROL   But how could I be. I was on the Pill.

NICKI   Told my boyfriend.

MEL   What did he say?

NICKI   We could get married.

CAROL   Typical of you.

ADELE   I'll give you the money.

MEL   Said he'd never have sex with me again.

CAROL   To get rid of it.

MEL   Or he was leaving.

ADELE   Good riddance!

ALL   Yes.

CAROL   But I didn't know for sure yet.

MEL   Bought a DIY kit?

ADELE   *Predictor?*

ALL   *Predictor.*

CAROL   Sounds like Russell Grant.

MEL   Well, fellow stargazers, there'll be a lost period in the early part of the month, but don't succumb under the pressure my loves, because there's sunny days ahead. Lots of sunshine.

NICKI   Went to Boots.

CAROL	I was embarrassed buying it.
ADELE	Went all red.
MEL	They're always next to the Durex.
NICKI	And whispering assistants.
MEL	Bet she's not married.
CAROL	Pretended I was married.
ADELE	Looking forward to the result.
CAROL	Always wanted a baby. But not yet. Asked my best friend to hit me in the stomach.
MEL	Did loads of strenuous exercise.
ALL	Touch and stretch, and touch and stretch.
CAROL	Thought about having a hot bath with a bottle of gin.
CAROL	And then the test.
MEL	Early morning.
NICKI	Felt quite sick.
ADELE	Oh God, it's a sign.
CAROL	Went to the toilet with my test-tube.
NICKI	Don't they make them small.
MEL	Shouldn't do—they cost enough.
ADELE	I know.
CAROL	Couldn't pee in it without getting it all over my hands.
ALL	Ugggh.
NICKI	Three drops of this.
MEL	Three drops of that.
ADELE	Give it a shake.
CAROL	And wait for the result.
ALL	Agony.
CAROL	I dared myself to look.
NICKI	Was dreading the result.

MEL	There's no room for a baby.
ADELE	It's not all my fault.
CAROL	But look...
NICKI	It's clear.
MEL	It's clear.
ADELE	No need to panic.
NICKI	No need to worry.
CAROL	Your body's your own again for another month at least.

(*They all laugh.*)

ADELE	(*to* MEL) Do you feel better now?
MEL	A bit.
CAROL	Don't let him use you.
NICKI	No.
MEL	I won't. I'll tell him. I'll tell him tomorrow.
ADELE	Yes.
CAROL	Come on. Cheer up.
NICKI	Yes. Let's have a smile.
MEL	"Ting"

SCENE THIRTEEN

ADELE	(*as if spotting someone*) Oh no! Look!
ALL	Oh! Bloody hell!
CAROL	(*as if Alan Whicker*) Yes, whenever you're relaxing behind the bar, in they come... "The posers".

(*The others strike up affected poses.* CAROL *continues narrating as if Alan Whicker.*)

| ALL | Darling— (*Changing pose.*) |

CAROL	Young couples in the early twenties, cavorting their wealth and youth with gay abandon. Aesthetes of Oscar Wilde's world here in the Eighties.
ALL	Lovey— (*Changing pose.*)
CAROL	Fast cars, fast bars, fast relationships and fast food.
ALL	Chuchee— (*Changing pose.*)
CAROL	Smelling like next year's French perfume and looking like Victoria Principal's sister — and that's just the boys. The ability to look like you've just stepped out of a magazine for women costing more than a pound, is just one of the many facilities they have at their fingertips. Others include talking garbage...
ALL	Terribly, terribly, terribly, terribly...
CAROL	Talking loud...
ALL	Awfully, awfully, awfully, awfully...
CAROL	And having no political acumen whatsoever...
ALL	Maggie, Maggie, Maggie, Maggie...

(*During the next sequence* CAROL *joins the others as yet another poser. They create a tableau of various posers' postures, speak their lines and then change posture. This happens repeatedly.*)

ADELE	She hasn't got a degree to her name and she married a gynaecologist.
ALL	Really!
CAROL	Nina told me that she thought Adrian Mole was a spy thriller.
ALL	Really!
MEL	He wrote it off on a bad corner, but his daddy said he'd pick up the bill.
ALL	Really!
NICKI	Some of the pickets were throwing stones at the police horses.
ALL	Oh, the poor things.

(*Change of lights and music as we move into the next scene.*)

SCENE FOURTEEN

(CAROL *and* MEL *are seated at two chairs. They will become* MR *and* MRS TRENDY. NICKI *serves at the bar.* ADELE *takes their order.*

ADELE   One tired waitress

CAROL   One trendy couple

MEL   In deep-fried love

          (CAROL *and* MEL *look at the menu.*)

MEL   Oh look at the menu. It's shaped like a cocktail
          shaker. Isn't that clever?

CAROL   That's why it's called *Shakers.*

          (*They laugh.*)

MEL   That's right. What do you fancy, darling?

CAROL   I dunno.

ADELE   Excuse me. Are you ready to order?

CAROL   We haven't had time to look at the menu.

ADELE   Okay sir, thank you. (*Aside*) Twat.

MEL   I don't know where to start.

ADELE   I think I've pulled a bad straw.

NICKI   Oh yes?

ADELE   Table six.

NICKI   They look like a nice couple.

ADELE   Nice. Very nice. Jesus, these shoes.

          (*A freeze: as* ADELE *stands upstage,* CAROL *and* MEL
          gesture that they want some service.)

MEL   Excuse me, excuse me.

          (ADELE *walks over.*)

ADELE   Ready to order, sir?

CAROL   Yes, we'd like to start with garlic sweetcorn.

ADELE   Sir.

MEL	No. I want the paté.
CAROL	Do you have any paté?
ADELE	Sir.
MEL	What sort of paté do you have?
ADELE	(*aside*) What sort do you want you silly looking gett?
MEL	Sorry?
ADELE	Duck paté. Liver paté.
MEL	I'll have the duck.
CAROL	One garlic sweetcorn, one duck paté; I'll have the lasagne; and Bev?
MEL	Could I um, ah, have the fillet?
ADELE	French fries, side salad or baked potato?
MEL	Sorry?
ADELE	(*aside*) Are you flaming deaf? Chips, lettuce or jacket spuds?
MEL	Could I have the side salad?
ADELE	Certainly. Any wine, sir?
MEL	Oh wine, wine.
CAROL	Yes, wine.
ADELE	(*aside*) It's on the back of the bloody menu.
CAROL	Ah ah. Here it is. I think we'll take the House white.
ADELE	Large carafe sir?
CAROL	I think so, don't you?
ADELE	(*aside*) You're paying for it. (*To audience*) And yet on the other hand, there is always the couple who are not *au courant*.
	(CAROL *and* MEL *remain seated. They become* MR *and* MRS UNTRENDY.)
MEL	Menu's good innit?
CAROL	What's it supposed to be?
MEL	What do you fancy?

CAROL	Sommat. I'm starved.
ADELE	Excuse me sir, are you ready to order?
CAROL	Giz a minute love.
ADELE	Okay sir, thank you.
MEL	I dun't know where to start.
ADELE	Another bad straw.
NICKI	Oh yeah?
ADELE	Table seven.
NICKI	They look like a nice couple.
ADELE	Nice? Jesus, I'm crippled.
CAROL	(*gesturing to* ADELE.) Oy!
ADELE	Ready to order sir?
CAROL	Yes I want garlic sweetcorn.
ADELE	Sir.
MEL	I'll have payt please.
ADELE	Payt?
MEL	Yeah. Duck payt.
ADELE	Certainly.
CAROL	And two lasag nees. And some white wine.
ADELE	Would either of you like French fries?
CAROL	French, with Italian? No thank you, love.
	(*Music*)

SCENE FIFTEEN

ADELE	Things are very hot
NICKI	Getting pretty hectic
CAROL	Behind the bar or in the kitchen

MEL	Palms are sweating, feet are itchin'
ADELE	Every order is served with a smile
ALL	Cheers!
NICKI	Every bad joke returned with panache
ALL	Oh that's really funny.
	(*A beat.*)
ALL	Yawn
ADELE	Bank holiday and the place is heaving
NICKI	The only room is on the ceiling. One *Blue Bols,* one *Sidecar.*
CAROL	*Banana Monster.*
	(NICKI *and* CAROL *take a seat.*)
ADELE	I think I've got this wrong.
MEL	You what?
ADELE	I've got an *Havana Zombie* mixed up with a *Salty Dog.*
MEL	What are you making?
ADELE	It's supposed to be a *Gin Sling.*
MEL	Oh shit!
ADELE	I've wasted loads of booze. I've got all the names mixed up in my head.
MEL	Good work.
ADELE	What am I gonna do?
MEL	Who is it for?
ADELE	That posh couple over there.
	(NICKI *and* CAROL *become the posh couple and wave.*)
ADELE	Oh God they've seen me.
MEL	Just give it her, it looks a nice colour.
ADELE	Doesn't look much like a *Gin Sling* though, does it?
MEL	Say it's a Special.
ADELE	A special what?

MEL I don't know. Make something up.

   (ADELE *takes the cocktail to the waiting posh couple.*)

ADELE Excuse me, Madam. Your cocktail. Sorry about the wait.

CAROL I ordered a *Gin Sling,* dear.

ADELE I know.

CAROL Fine. Take that away.

ADELE Well you see, you're our hundredth customer tonight, so you win the Surprise Cocktail.

CAROL But we've only recently arrived and the place is seething.

ADELE Hundredth Cocktail customer, I mean.

CAROL Oh.

NICKI Oh great. Thank you.

ADELE Yes, so you get the Surprise Cocktail.

CAROL What's in it?

ADELE That's the surprise.

CAROL What's it called then?

ADELE Er...um...(ADELE *looks round for inspiration.*) Oh, er, *Emergency Exit.*

CAROL Oh, potent is it?

NICKI I'm sure they make up these ridiculous names on the spur of the moment. You couldn't make me *Two Hind Legs of an Elephant,* could you?

   (*They laugh.*)

CAROL Oh, Gerald!

ADELE (*aside*) Don't be so smart, you silly looking bastard.

NICKI Sorry?

ADELE I'm afraid I don't know that one.

NICKI It was a joke. (*She laughs. Pause. Then she suddenly remembers that she has forgotten to sing "Happy Birthday" to the birthday group.*) Oh no!!!

   (*The girls form the "Shakers motif" and sing "Happy Birthday".*)

SCENE SIXTEEN

When they finish singing MEL, CAROL *and* ADELE *sit down and become the animated birthday girls once more.*

MEL   Oh, that's smashing. Where did you get it?

CAROL   C & A.

MEL   God, it's great is that.

ADELE   It's nice here, int it?

MEL   Haven't you been here before?

ADELE   No.

MEL   God, it's great.

ADELE   Packed innit?

CAROL   My face is on fire.

ADELE   You'll be alright.

NICKI   And for a birthday treat, a cocktail with a sparkler in it. Very, very neat. (*She approaches their table.*)

ALL   Oh int it nice? Lovely. It's great. (*They all hiccup.*)

ADELE   Hey?

CAROL   What?

ADELE   Can you see Andy King?

CAROL   Can I hell—it's chock-a-block.

MEL   I feel a bit tipsy. It's this wine. I'm not used to it.

ADELE   I've had a monster *Pina Colada*. I feel great.

CAROL   Hey watch this. A party popper.

             (*The miming of a party popper presents great fun as we see them explode in the air.*)

MEL   It's great. Hey look at that table? Wave at them?

CAROL   Hey up oooooohhh!!!!

ADELE   It's her birthday?

MEL   Twenty-one, you cheeky sods.

NICKI	Hey. Crackers.
ALL	Oooohhh yehhhhh!!!!
	(*They mime the pulling of crackers, put on the hats, etc.*)
MEL	Oh, I've got a ring.
ALL	Uuurrmm...
ADELE	I've got a hat. It's daft.
MEL	Hey, it suits you.
CAROL	Hey, listen to this. ''The more you take the more you leave behind.'' What is it?
ADELE	Tablets?
MEL	Water?
NICKI	What?
CAROL	Steps, the more steps.
ALL	Oh yeah, good that.
CAROL	A toast to Mand. Twenty-one today.
ADELE	God bless you, love.
	(*They all sing one verse of ''Twenty-one today''.*)

SCENE SEVENTEEN

The girls are all moving around the stage at great speed. The atmosphere is hectic. They alternately play the roles of waitresses and customers.

CAROL	Excuse me, love.
MEL	One *Sidecar?*
CAROL	Excuse me. I ordered a fillet, not sirloin.
NICKI	Seafood pasta?
ADELE	Another round of garlic bread was it over here?
NICKI	Can we have another bottle of *Liebfraumilch?*
CAROL	Yes in a moment, sir.

MEL	I haven't had my starter yet, love.
ADELE	Garlic mushrooms?
NICKI	This bread's cold, love. I said this bread is cold.
CAROL	Two *Blue Bols* and a brandy?
NICKI	Could we see the menu?
CAROL	Excuse me.
MEL	Watch your backs, please.
ADELE	Waitress?
NICKI	Watch the floor it's slippery.

(CAROL *falls and the drinks fly in all directions. The tone is one of general panic.* CAROL *is shaken and upset.*)

MEL	Are you alright?
CAROL	Yeah.
MEL	Sure?
CAROL	Feel dizzy.
ADELE	She okay?
MEL	Think so.
ADELE	Get her up.
CAROL	I'm boiling.
ADELE	She's okay.
CAROL	Sorry about the mess, sir.
NICKI	Is she alright?
MEL	Think so.
NICKI	Are you alright Carol?
CAROL	Yeah.
NICKI	Jesus it's stupid in here tonight.
CAROL	I'll be okay...okay...I'm fine. I just slipped.
NICKI	I'll clear that up for you.

(*Music*)

SCENE EIGHTEEN

MEL   I don't think it's fair, that's all.

ADELE   What isn't?

MEL   Well, she's having a day off to go down there for that audition. It's just a waste of time in any case.

ADELE   Oh don't be like that.

MEL   Well I can't help it.

ADELE   It might be her big break.

MEL   We've got to cover for her, haven't we. If we had a day off, he'd want to know why.

CAROL   Nicki never has time off.

MEL   She's always late on Mondays though. She sings in a club, Sunday nights.

ADELE   What's it to do with you?

MEL   Well singing in a club...it's degrading.

CAROL   You've got some funny ideas.

MEL   She'll never make an actress.

CAROL   Why?

MEL   Her nose is too big.

ADELE   I say good luck to her.

CAROL   And me.

MEL   She'll be back here tomorrow with her tail between her legs.

CAROL   At least she's had a go.

ADELE   Do you think she's got a chance?

CAROL   Honest?

ADELE   Yeah, honest.

CAROL   No, not really.

ADELE   Oh I feel right sorry for her.

CAROL   She got guts though.

ADELE　　I wouldn't have the nerve to stand up in front of
　　　　　people, me.

CAROL　　Why not? You do it every night in here.

ADELE　　Oh yeah. I think I might apply. (*To audience.*) Nicki's
　　　　　first audition—

SCENE NINETEEN

Spotlight on NICKI

NICKI　　My first audition. God I'm nervous. Do I look
　　　　　nervous? Well I am. God, I'm shakin' like a leaf. I'm
　　　　　ready though. Got all my stuff. The expense, shit.
　　　　　Twenty quid return and eighteen quid to audition.
　　　　　Carol thinks I've got a chance and she should know.

CAROL　　You've got a chance.

NICKI　　I don't know why I want to act; well I mean I do.
　　　　　Everybody has a dream, I suppose. I love all the old
　　　　　films and that. They make me feel really good
　　　　　somehow. And you see I'm not from a theatrical
　　　　　family. My dad drives a bus.

ADELE　　Fares please.

NICKI　　And my mam works on school dinners.

CAROL　　More potatoes, love.

NICKI　　Trouble is, to be honest, nobody from our end knows
　　　　　how to help you. I mean, I'm twenty-one and I still
　　　　　want to act. It's taken me three years to get an
　　　　　audition together. I hope I don't blow it. I've read
　　　　　some books and that. I'm not thick, but I think plays
　　　　　are boring.

ALL　　　Shhh...

NICKI　　I watch a lot of videos. Hey I watched that *Educating
　　　　　Rita*. Have you seen it? Ooh it's good, but she said
　　　　　that *Macbeth* was great. I got a copy from the library;
　　　　　I think it's boring... Oh well, keep your fingers
　　　　　crossed for me, and your legs and anything else you
　　　　　can cross.

(*The lights come up.* ADELE, CAROL *and* MEL *become three hopefuls, sitting on a line of chairs, waiting to be called for the audition.*)

ADELE   Hi!

CAROL   Hi ya!

NICKI   Hello.

ADELE   Have you come for the audition?

NICKI   Yeah.

ADELE   I'm Jackie.

CAROL   I'm Claire.

MEL   Louise. Hi there.

NICKI   Hello...I'm Nicola Bostock, Nicki.

ALL   Hi.

NICKI   Do I look nervous?

MEL   No, why?

NICKI   Oh nothing really. I just wondered, really, if I looked nervous coz I'm not...

CAROL   Is this your first audition?

NICKI   Yeah, I've come on the train. I work in a cocktail bar. Well, it's my job. *Shakers*, it's called. I'm twenty-one. (*A long silence.*) Have you all been to auditions before then?

MEL   This is my second year of trying. Last year they said I was too young. I had a recall at the Old Vic.

NICKI   Oh.

ADELE   I'm just doing RADA, mainly to say that I've done it.

CAROL   Where are you from?

NICKI   North.

CAROL   Birmingham?

NICKI   Well I was born in Bradford.

ALL   Oh.

NICKI	Are you all from London?
ADELE	I was born in Looe, but I live in Colchester.
MEL	We're both from London.
	(*Another silence.*)
NICKI	God, I'm really nervous.
MEL	You'll get used to it.
NICKI	I hope not. It costs a fortune.
ADELE	You have prepared a speech, haven't you?
NICKI	Have I! They've asked me to do a speech, a song and a dance.
CAROL	I'm doing Beatrice from *Much Ado*, Nina from *The Seagull* and Wilkomen.
NICKI	I love that.
CAROL	*The Seagull?*
NICKI	No *Cabaret*. Wilkomen, bienvenue, welcome.
ADELE	I'm doing Lady Macbeth, Juliet if they want it, Laura from *The Glass Menagerie* and Hedda Gabler.
NICKI	Aren't you doing a song?
ADELE	"L'Oiseau rebelle" from Bizet's *Carmen*.
NICKI	Oh great!
MEL	I'm doing Alison Porter, Ophelia, Charlotte Corday from *Marat Sade* and Richard III. And for a song I'm doing "As long as he needs me."
NICKI	*Oliver?*
MEL	Yes.
NICKI	That's brilliant.
MEL	My singing teacher thinks it suits me.
CAROL	What are you doing, Nicki?
	(*Suddenly the lights change and we are into* NICKI's *audition.*)
NICKI	I'm doing a speech, but it's not from a play.

ALL   Ohh!

NICKI   It is something that I've put together myself. Er...I've
           written all the words down on a bit of paper so you
           can test me. Yeah. Right. It's called *"The Smile"*.
           (*Pause.*) Right I'll start shall I? (*Pause.*) I'm a bit
           nervous, so it might be a bit shit. She'd been in
           hospital for about four days. She was seventy. She
           went into hospital for an hysterectomy; the operation
           had been a great success. I went to see her and she
           looked great, she even showed me the stitches. She's
           my gran, by the way. So at work, I was having a
           laugh and a good time. Then they rang, the hospital,
           said she'd had a stroke. So I went on the bus to the
           hospital, I felt sick, travelling all that way on a bus.
           She was on the sixth floor, I remember that, in a side
           cubicle in a ward full of old ladies. I walked into the
           room. My mam and dad were looking out of the
           window, looking across the parkland of the hospital.
           And my uncle and auntie were there, looking out of
           the window; they were crying. My gran was laid in
           bed; half of her face was blue and deformed, her
           mouth was all twisted and taut, one eye was closed.
           She looked at me, and tried to smile. I remember the
           crying in the background. She tried to speak, but said
           nothing. She just laid there. "Hello gran," I said.
           "Hello. What's all this bloody nonsense about having
           a stroke? Eh?" And she just smiled at me. She just
           smiled.
           (*Music*)

SCENE TWENTY

*We are back with the birthday girls at Shakers. Three chairs
represent three toilets. NICKI is seated on one chair, crying.
MELANIE is at the mirror. Enter CAROL and ADELE.*

CAROL   Ooh. Nice toilets.

ADELE   Always a queue.

CAROL   You go first.

ADELE	I'm dying. Are you?
CAROL	There's one, Shaz. Susan's coming out.
MEL	Hi ya!
ADELE	Come in with me.
CAROL	What for?
ADELE	A chat.
CAROL	Get lost.

(ADELE *enters the toilet.*)

ADELE	Hey. It's alright in here.
CAROL	What did you expect?
ADELE	Nice seats.
CAROL	Shut up and get on with it.
ADELE	I am.
CAROL	I think this one's out of order.

(NICKI *exits from the toilet crying.*)

NICKI	Sorry Tracey, it won't flush.
CAROL	Thanks. What's up with her?
MEL	Don't know.

(CAROL *enters the toilet.* NICKI *goes as if to dry her hands.*)

CAROL	(*as if banging on the wall.*) I'm in here now Shaz.
ADELE	Have you got any paper?
CAROL	Yes. Do you want some?
ADELE	Yes, please.
CAROL	I'll bung it underneath.
ADELE	You'd think they'd have paper in here, wouldn't you. It's nearly as bad as them toilets at the bus station.
CAROL	Ding ding. Ta-ra.

(*Scene changes to the bus station.* ADELE *runs in, desperate to find a toilet.* MEL *and* CAROL *become the toilet attendants,* MADGE *and* FLO.)

ADELE   Thank God. I thought I'd never get to a loo in time. I've been on that bus for chuffin' ages. Two hours they said, it was nearer bloody three! I almost wet myself. Oh shit, five pence. Bloody cheek, five pence. (*She looks in her purse.*) 5p, 5p, 5p. Chuffin' hell, I can't find one. Oh beaut, somebody's coming out. (CAROL *exits.*) Thanks.

MEL   Let that door go!

ADELE   I'm bursting.

MEL   Let it shut!

(*Sound of door shutting.*)

ADELE   But I haven't any change.

MEL   Come here and I'll give you some.

ADELE   Oh hurry up.

MEL   Here.

ADELE   Thanks.

MEL   They make me bloody sick, Flo. Owt for nowt, I'm fed up with it, day in day out.

NICKI   I know, love. I know.

MEL   It's only soddin' 5p.

ADELE   5p for a pee, it's beyond me.

(*Scene returns to Shaker's toilets. The girls are now around the mirrors.* NICKI *is crying again.*)

NICKI   So she says to me, "If you don't keep your bloody hands off him I'll smack you."

MEL   Did she?

NICKI   As if I'm scared of her.

CAROL   She's a fart, that lass.

NICKI   But he'll probably go off with her.

ADELE   He won't.

NICKI   But what if he does, eh? But what if he does?

CAROL   Smack her.

MEL   Yes.

NICKI   I'll die if he leaves me.

CAROL   Will you chuff? God, these mirrors really show your
        spots up.

NICKI   I will.

ADELE   I look right pale.

NICKI   I couldn't bear it if he went off with her.

MEL   He's not that nice anyway. Can I borrow your comb?

CAROL   Yes here. My hair's dropped.

ADELE   It suits you like that.

CAROL   What a mess?

ADELE   No, that style.

CAROL   Got any hairspray?

MEL   I have, there's just a bit left.

NICKI   I mean she's really attractive, much nicer than me.

ADELE   She's not.

MEL   Get a few drinks down you and forget about him.

NICKI   I just want to die.

CAROL   I think I'm going to have another one of them
        cocktails.

ADELE   Yes they're nice aren't they?

MEL   They're mekking me feel dizzy.

NICKI   Do you know something, I hate my face.

CAROL   Put a bag on your head.

NICKI   Oooaah...

        (*Music comes up as the girls become waitresses once more.*)

SCENE TWENTY-ONE

(*The waitresses are serving as* ADELE *enters.*)

ADELE   There's another girl crying in the toilets.

NICKI   Oh bloody hell.

ADELE   Over some bloke.

CAROL   Pathetic.

MEL   Is she drunk?

ADELE   Looks like it.

CAROL   You'd think they'd nothing better to do. As if getting a bloke's everything.

MEL   Well, I wouldn't mind a decent one.

CAROL   They're so young, ruled by their hearts and not their heads.

MEL   They're having a good time, what's wrong with that?

CAROL   Are they?

ADELE   Yes.

CAROL   I suppose there's nothing else really.

ADELE   What do you mean?

CAROL   Well it's either a shitty job like this or the dole queue, coming out getting drunk, having a laugh. It's something to do, isn't it?

NICKI   God, you're depressing.

CAROL   That's why they want a bloke, why they give in so easily, the promise of a future.

MEL   They're enjoying themselves, that's all.

CAROL   Yes, but look at them, they get a man and go in to the whole thing hoping that this time it will last. But nine times out of ten it doesn't, does it?

MEL   (*reflective*) No.

CAROL   They're used, 'cos men don't have the same pressures. It's alright for them to play around until they're thirty, forty even. But if a woman does that,

people think she's a freak. Anyway there's so much
more to life than that.

ADELE   You keep saying this Carol, but some people are
           happy like that. I mean I think my boyfriend's great.

CAROL   There's more to life than sleeping with somebody,
           Adele.

(*Spotlight on* ADELE.)

ADELE   I first slept with somebody when I was sixteen. Yeah,
           I know it's young. He was a teacher at school, so it
           seemed alright. Mr Coates, well Mike. He was really
           good looking, I thought he was great. We just sort of
           drifted together on a school trip. Nobody knew, it was
           a big secret that seemed to make it more special. He
           didn't force me to sleep with him, in fact he was
           really nice and sweet. The truth is, I fancied him that
           much I couldn't help it. God, I couldn't leave him
           alone, poor bloke. I was sensible though, so I
           thought. I tried to get on the pill but I had jaundice
           when I was a kid, so I ended up with a cap. I'm not
           kidding, they're a pain in the neck. I've got a coil
           now, it's okay. We went on holiday for two weeks to
           Scotland. My mam thought I was hostelling with my
           mates. I spoilt it though, typical, found out I was
           pregnant. To be honest I'd suspected for weeks but I
           kept putting it to the back of my mind. But it had got
           to the stage where I was sick. I didn't really think
           about it, I just asked for an abortion. I had it up
           there in Scotland, in a hospital by the sea. There were
           about eight of us in a ward, all the others had slippers
           and dressing gowns, and orange juice at the side of
           their beds. I had to make do with a hospital nightie,
           my stocking feet, and a baggy combat jumper I'd
           taken camping with me. It's soon done, you bleed a
           lot, feel depressed but it is a relief as well. I wanted to
           tell people, but I knew I'd better not. I mean the
           thing is, shall I tell Steve, my boyfriend? I mean,
           we're gerrin' engaged. And it can stop you having
           kids can't it? I'm frightened in case he leaves me. I
           think I'll keep it a secret, between me and you. Don't
           tell anyone, will you? Promise.

SCENE TWENTY-TWO

The four girls once more become the birthday party girls, doing the Conga.

ALL   Na na na na na na na na etc
We're getting very drunk now
We're getting very merry
Na na na na na na na na
Happy birthday Mandy
What a super party
Na na na na na na na na

ADELE   I've got my silly hat on

NICKI   I've got my party poppers

MEL   I've laddered all my stockings

CAROL   I've stuffed my face quite stupid

ALL   Na na na na na na na na... (*gradually fading out amidst shouts of "goodnight" and "come again soon".*)

SCENE TWENTY-THREE

The girls now recline for a moment at the bar. As they take a short rest there, they start to take off their shoes and begin to groan. We see that they are in the same positions as at the start of the play.

CAROL   Turn that bloody music off!

MEL   Yeah.

ADELE   Oh that's another thing. The music—

NICKI   It pulsates everywhere; the toilets, the bar, the kitchen...

CAROL   Some nights I wake up screaming the lyrics to Coco Cabana.

ADELE   Look at the mess; it's like an elephant's been sick.

ALL   Oooohhh!

(*Music begins to play in the background.*)

MEL	My legs are killing me.
CAROL	It's these bloody shoes.
ADELE	Do you still feel dizzy, Carol?
CAROL	No. I think it was the heat. I'm alright now.
NICKI	Jesus.
ADELE	(*taking her shoes off*) Oooh...
NICKI	I'm gonna see somebody about my feet.
CAROL	These are ridiculous.
NICKI	They're killing me.
MEL	And me. Put 'em away.
NICKI	Hey. Got another audition on Tuesday. I might not be here.
ADELE	Have you?
CAROL	Big break eh?
NICKI	Dunno? There's always a chance.
ADELE	Yes.
MEL	Right. I'm off.
CAROL	Take care.
ADELE	Yeah, see you.
ALL	See you.
CAROL	Hey watch yourself. (*To audience*) And at the end of all this, there's the long trek home.

(*The girls all exchange goodnights to each other.*)

SCENE TWENTY-FOUR — EPILOGUE

CAROL	Your footsteps resound in the dark
ADELE	And you're on your own
MEL	Alone in the night
NICKI	All dark. The pavestones wet and shiny

CAROL	As you walk, shadows
ADELE	In doorways
MEL	Noises
NICKI	Around corners
CAROL	Coming towards you, two dark figures
ADELE	Should you run?
MEL	They are coming straight for you
NICKI	You freeze to the spot

(*They stagger around as though they were drunks.*)

ALL	Goodnight love
CAROL	Goodnight
ADELE	It's alright
NICKI	Another few steps. A taxi in sight. I'll take a taxi. It's safer
MEL	In the back you climb...
CAROL	There's no one about
NICKI	Is he going the right way?
ADELE	Is he a taxi driver?
CAROL	Late at night and you've got in a car with a complete stranger
MEL	The fear doubles, gets larger
NICKI	Is he going the right way?
CAROL	I'll get out here thanks
MEL	Out you climb and pay your two quid...
ALL	Goodnight love. Night
ADELE	There's still a long walk
MEL	All is quiet
CAROL	All is still
ADELE	It's one o'clock in the morning
NICKI	Not a soul in sight

*MEL   Behind you...

CAROL   Footsteps

MEL   Getting closer

ADELE   You speed up

CAROL   Quicker

MEL   Behind you...

NICKI   The footsteps get louder...

*CAROL   Nearer

          (*The section between asterisks is repeated three times building
          to a climax.)

NICKI   (to ADELE) Here you are love, you forgot your gloves.

ADELE   Oh thanks.

NICKI   Goodnight.

ALL   Goodnight.

          (As the last number comes up, the four girls form the
          "Smiling motif" rather pathetically. Bow.)

ONE OF US

ROBIN CHAPMAN

What really happened during that summer weekend in 1951 when Guy Burgess and Donald Maclean suddenly disappeared only to surface later in Moscow?

One of Us sets out to unravel the story behind Burgess's dramatic defection to Russia, at the same time presenting a completely new perspective on a fascinating and extraordinary series of events. The play focuses upon Goronwy Rees, whose calm and settled life is overturned by a visit from his old university friend, the flamboyant extrovert, Guy Burgess. It is Rees's crisis of conscience, in the face of E.M. Forster's declaration that he would rather betray his country than his friends, that forms the pivot around which a tense and compelling drama develops.

Ultimately, who is left feeling the real traitor?

For further information, contact Warner Chappell Plays, 129 Park Street, London W1Y 3FA.

PRINCIPIA SCRIPTORIAE

RICHARD NELSON

Principia Scriptoriae opens in 1970 in a Latin American country where two aspiring young writers, one American, the other Latin American, meet when they are thrown into prison for distributing subversive leaflets. The second part of the play is set fifteen years later when the right-wing dictatorship has been replaced by a left-wing revolutionary government. The political tables have turned and the 'principles of writing' have now ironically altered. The two men find themselves on opposite sides of a conference table bargaining for the release of a poet held by the new leftist government.

Within this context Richard Nelson explores and questions the relationship between the two men when principles of a more creative and personal nature are undermined by the pressures of political posturing and literary ambition.

'A passionate, enlightened and altogether admirable play' *Time Magazine*
'A brilliant study of two young men' *Guardian*

For further information, contact Warner Chappell Plays, 129 Park Street, London W1Y 3FA.

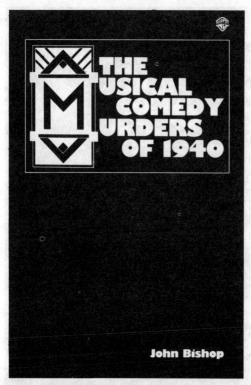

THE MUSICAL COMEDY MURDERS OF 1940

John Bishop

Under the guise of a backer's audition for their new musical, the production team of a recent Broadway flop assemble at an isolated country mansion to try to piece together the identity of the mysterious "Stage Door Slasher", who murdered three of the chorus girls in the show. While a blizzard rages outside and the composer, lyricist, director and actors prepare for their performances, the Slasher reappears, striking again — and again, and again!

Assassins stalk each other through secret passageways and behind hidden library panels in an ever-increasing romp through comic pastiche involving German spies, a bumbling police investigator and a maid who is apparently four different people — all of which figure in the intrigue and hilarity before the Slasher is finally unmasked!

"The fun manages to be almost as plentiful as the bodies."
Evening Standard

"Imagine a 42nd Street with corpses where the songs ought to be."
Punch

"The effect is phenomenal and blinding — Take Shades." *Observer*

For further information contact Warner Chappell Plays Ltd, 129 Park Street, London WlY 3FA. Telephone 01-629-7600.

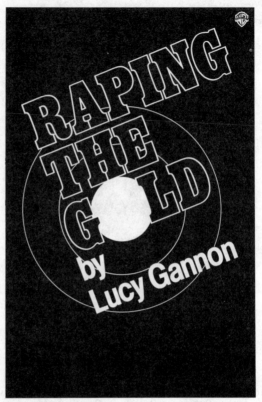

Set on and around an archery field in a small Derbyshire town beset by the closure of the local factory works, the metaphor of an arrow splitting the golden centre of an archer's target emphasizes the way in which long term unemployment shatters the dreams and ideas of a community torn apart by events beyond their control.

This powerful and moving play contrasts the hopes and despair of friends and family within the community, uncompromising in their personal beliefs. *Raping The Gold*'s warm sense of humour is complemented by a fierce compassion for individuals whose lives are caught between a betrayed past and an abandoned future, where for some the local archery club is the only source of solace and inspiration left available.

"It is a work of outstanding talent." *Sunday Times*

"Ms Gannon has a powerful sense of place and mood ... Her great gift is the capacity to convey desolation through resonant images." *The Guardian*

For further information contact Warner Chappell Plays Ltd, 129 Park Street, London W1Y 3FA. Telephone 01-629-7600.

ASYLUM

Paul Kember

When a film crew descend on a decaying Victorian psychiatric hospital to shoot a pop video for a would-be hit single, both the inmates of the hospital and the film crew are thrown into chaos by the return of a former mental patient who has been discharged into 'community care'. When it emerges that her return is for more than a friendly visit, the events that follow are both deeply humorous and tragic as *Asylum* exposes the immorality of the film industry while at the same time showing that the gap between sanity and abnormality is precariously thin.

"It is not easy to write a comedy about the present day inmates of a Victorian lunatic asylum, but Kember has succeeded." *Sunday Telegraph*.

For further information, contact Warner Chappell Plays, 129 Park Street, London W1Y 3FA. Telephone 01-629 7600.